RELIGIONS OF THE WORLD

BUDDHISM

CHRISTIANITY

CONFUCIANISM

HINDUISM

INDIGENOUS RELIGIONS

ISLAM

JUDAISM

NEW RELIGIONS

SHINTO

SIKHISM

TAOISM

RELIGIONS
OF THE
WORLD

DISCARD

BUDDHISM

Leslie D. Alldritt
Associate Professor of Religion and Philosophy
Northland College

Series Consulting Editor **Ann Marie B. Bahr**
Professor of Religious Studies,
South Dakota State University

Foreword by **Martin E. Marty**
Professor Emeritus,
University of Chicago Divinity School

CHELSEA HOUSE
PUBLISHERS
A Haights Cross Communications Company
Philadelphia

FRONTIS: There are approximately 360 million Buddhists worldwide, most living on the continent of Asia. The countries with the largest per-capita population of Buddhists are Thailand (95 percent) and Cambodia (90 percent).

CHELSEA HOUSE PUBLISHERS

VP, NEW PRODUCT DEVELOPMENT Sally Cheney
DIRECTOR OF PRODUCTION Kim Shinners
CREATIVE MANAGER Takeshi Takahashi
MANUFACTURING MANAGER Diann Grasse

Staff for BUDDHISM

EXECUTIVE EDITOR Lee Marcott
EDITOR Christian Green
PRODUCTION EDITOR Noelle Nardone
ASSOCIATE PHOTO EDITOR Noelle Nardone
SERIES AND COVER DESIGNER Keith Trego
LAYOUT 21st Century Publishing and Communications, Inc.

A Haights Cross Communications ◀ Company

www.chelseahouse.com

First Printing

9 8 7 6 5 4 3 2 1

Library of Congress Cataloging-in-Publication Data

Alldritt, Leslie D.
   Buddhism / Leslie D. Alldritt.
      p. cm.—(Religions of the world)
Includes bibliographical references and index.
   ISBN 0-7910-7855-8 (alk. paper) — ISBN 0-7910-8354-3 (pbk.)
   1. Buddhism. I. Title. II. Series.
BQ4012.A55 2004
294.3—dc22

                                        2004011864

All links and web adresses were checked and verified to be correct at the time of publication. Because of the dynamic nature of the web, some addresses and links may have changed since publication and may no longer be valid.

CONTENTS

Foreword

Martin E. Marty

On this very day, like all other days, hundreds of millions of people around the world will turn to religion for various purposes.

On the one hand, there are purposes that believers in any or all faiths, as well as unbelievers, might regard as positive and benign. People turn to religion or, better, to their own particular faith, for the experience of healing and to inspire acts of peacemaking. They want to make sense of a world that can all too easily overwhelm them because it so often seems to be meaningless and even absurd. Religion then provides them with beauty, inspires their souls, and impels them to engage in acts of justice and mercy.

To be informed citizens of our world, readers have good reason to learn about these features of religions that mean so much to so many. Those who study the faiths do not have to agree with any of them and could not agree with all of them, different as they are. But they need basic knowledge of religions to understand other people and to work out strategies for living with them.

On the other hand—and religions always have an "other hand"—believers in any of the faiths, and even unbelievers who are against all of them, will find their fellow humans turning to their religions for purposes that seem to contradict all those positive features. Just as religious people can heal and be healed, they can also kill or be killed in the name of faith. So it has been through history.

This killing can be literal: Most armed conflicts and much terrorism today are inspired by the stories, commands, and promises that come along with various faiths. People can and do read and act upon scriptures that can breed prejudice and that lead them to reject other beliefs and believers. Or the killing can be figurative, which means that faiths can be deadening to the spirit. In the name of faith, many people are repressed, oppressed, sometimes victimized and abused.

If religion can be dangerous and if it may then come with "Handle with Care" labels, people who care for their own security, who want to lessen tensions and inspire concord, have to equip themselves by learning something about the scriptures and stories of their own and other faiths. And if they simply want to take delight in human varieties and imaginings, they will find plenty to please them in lively and reliable accounts of faiths.

A glance at television or at newspapers and magazines on almost any day will reveal stories that display one or both sides of religion. However, these stories usually have to share space with so many competing accounts, for example, of sports and enter-tainment or business and science, that writers and broadcasters can rarely provide background while writing headlines. Without such background, it is hard to make informed judgments.

The series RELIGIONS OF THE WORLD is designed to provide not only background but also rich illustrative material about the foreground, presenting the many features of faiths that are close at hand. Whoever reads all the volumes in the series will find that these religions have some elements in common. Overall, one can deduce that their followers take certain things with ultimate seriousness: human dignity, devotion to the sacred, the impulse to live a moral life. Yet few people are inspired by religions in general. They draw strength from what they hold particularly. These particulars of each faith are not always contradictory to those of others, but they are different in important ways. It is simply a fact that believers are informed and inspired by stories told in separate and special ways.

A picture might make all this vivid: Reading about a religion, visiting a place of worship, or coming into the company of those who believe in and belong to a particular faith, is like entering a room. Religions are, in a sense, spiritual "furnished apartments." Their adherents have placed certain pictures on the wall and moved in with their own kind of furnishings, having developed their special ways of receiving or blocking out light from such places. Some of their figurative apartments are airy, and some stress strength and security.

Philosopher George Santayana once wrote that, just as we do not speak language, we speak particular languages, so we have religion not as a whole but as religions "in particular." The power of each living and healthy religion, he added, consists in "its special and surprising message and in the bias which that revelation gives to life." Each creates "another world to live in."

The volumes in this series are introductions to several spiritual furnished apartments, guides to the special and surprising messages of these large and complex communities of faith, or religions. These are not presented as a set of items in a cafeteria line down which samplers walk, tasting this, rejecting that, and moving on. They are not bids for window-shoppers or shoppers of any sort, though it may be that a person without faith might be drawn to one or another expression of the religions here described. The real intention of the series is to educate.

Education could be dull and drab. Picture a boring professor standing in front of a class and droning on about distant realities. The authors in this series, however, were chosen because they can bring readers up close to faiths and, sometimes better, to people of faith; not to religion but to people who are religious in particular ways.

As one walks the streets of a great metropolis, it is not easy and may not even be possible to deduce the faith-commitments of those one passes unless they wear a particular costume—some garb or symbol prescribed by their faith. Therefore, while passing them by, it is not likely that one can learn much about the dreams and hopes, the fears and intentions, of those around them.

These books, in effect, stop the procession of passersby and bid visitors to enter those sanctuaries where communities worship. Each book could serve as a guide to worship. Several years ago, a book called *How to Be a Perfect Stranger* offered brief counsel on how to feel and to be at home among worshipers from other traditions. This series recognizes that we are not strangers to each other only in sanctuaries. We carry over our attachments to conflicting faiths where we go to work or vote or serve in the military or have fun. These "carryovers" tend to come from the basic stories and messages of the several faiths.

The publishers have taken great pains to assign their work to authors of a particular sort. Had these been anti-religious or anti–the religion about which they write, they would have done a disservice. They would, in effect, have been blocking the figurative doors to the faiths or smashing the furniture in the sanctuaries. On the other hand, it would be wearying and distorting had the assignment gone to public relations agents, advertisers who felt called to claim "We're Number One!" concerning the faith about which they write.

Fair-mindedness and accuracy are the two main marks of these authors. In rather short compass, they reach a wide range of subjects, focusing on everything one needs to advance basic understanding. Their books are like mini-encyclopedias, full of information. They introduce the holidays that draw some neighbors to be absent from work or school for a day or a season. They include galleries of notable figures in each faith-community.

Since most religions in the course of history develop different ways in the many diverse places where they thrive, or because they attract intelligent, strong-willed leaders and writers, they come up with different emphases. They divide and split off into numberless smaller groups: Protestant and Catholic and Orthodox Christians, Shiite and Sunni Muslims, Orthodox and Reform Jews, and many kinds of Buddhists and Hindus. The writers in this series do justice to these variations, providing a kind of map without which one will get lost in the effort to understand.

Some years ago, a rabbi friend, Samuel Sandmel, wrote a book about his faith called *The Enjoyment of Scripture*. What an astonishing concept, some might think: After all, religious scriptures deal with desperately urgent, life-and-death-and-eternity issues. They have to be grim and those who read them likewise. Not so. Sandmel knew what the authors of this series also know and impart: The journeys of faith and the encounter with the religions of others include pleasing and challenging surprises. I picture many a reader coming across something on these pages that at first looks obscure or forbidding, but then, after a slightly longer look, makes sense and inspires an "aha!" There are many occasions for "aha-ing!" in these books. One can also wager that many a reader will come away from the encounters thinking, "I never knew that!" or "I never thought of that before." And they will be more ready than they had been to meet strangers of other faiths in a world that so many faiths *have* to share, or that they *get* to share.

Martin E. Marty
The University of Chicago

Preface

Ann Marie B. Bahr

The majority of people, both in the United States and around the world, consider religion to be an important part of their lives. Beyond its significance in individual lives, religion also plays an important role in war and peace, politics, social policy, ethics, and cultural expression. Yet few people feel well-prepared to carry on a conversation about religion with friends, colleagues, or their congressional delegation. The amount of knowledge people have about their own faith varies, but very few can lay claim to a solid understanding of a religion other than their own. As the world is drawn closer together by modern communications, and the religions of the world jostle each other in religiously plural societies, the lack of our ability to dialogue about this aspect of our lives results in intercultural conflict rather than cooperation. It means that individuals of different religious persuasions will either fight about their faiths or avoid the topic of religion altogether. Neither of these responses aids in the building of healthy, religiously plural societies. This gap in our knowledge is therefore significant, and grows increasingly more significant as religion plays a larger role in national and international politics.

The authors and editors of this series are dedicated to the task of helping to prepare present and future decision-makers to deal with religious pluralism in a healthy way. The objective scholarship found in these volumes will blunt the persuasive power of popular misinformation. The time is short, however. Even now, nations are dividing along religious lines, and "neutral" states as well as partisan religious organizations are precariously, if not always intentionally, tipping delicate balances of power in favor of one religious group or another with doles of aid and support for certain policies or political leaders. Intervention in the affairs of other nations is always a risky business, but doing it without understanding of the religious sensitivities of the populace dramatically increases the chances that even well-intentioned intervention will be perceived as political coercion or cultural invasion. With such signs of ignorance already manifest, the day of reckoning for educational policies that ignore the study of the world's religions cannot be far off.

This series is designed to bring religious studies scholarship to the leaders of today and tomorrow. It aims to answer the questions that students, educators, policymakers, parents, and citizens might have about the new religious milieu in which we find ourselves. For example, a person hearing about a religion that is foreign to him or her might want answers to questions like these:

- How many people believe in this religion? What is its geographic distribution? When, where, and how did it originate?

- What are its beliefs and teachings? How do believers worship or otherwise practice their faith?

- What are the primary means of social reinforcement? How do believers educate their youth? What are their most important communal celebrations?

- What are the cultural expressions of this religion? Has it inspired certain styles of art, architecture, literature, or music? Conversely, does it avoid art, literature, or music for religious reasons? Is it associated with elements of popular culture?

- How do the people who belong to this religion remember the past? What have been the most significant moments in their history?

- What are the most salient features of this religion today? What is likely to be its future?

We have attempted to provide as broad coverage as possible of the various religious forces currently shaping the planet. Judaism, Christianity, Islam, Hinduism, Buddhism, Confucianism, Taoism, Sikhism, and Shinto have each been allocated an entire volume. In recognition of the fact that many smaller ancient and new traditions also exercise global influence, we present coverage of some of these in two additional volumes titled "Indigenous Religions" and "New Religions." Each volume in the series discusses demographics and geography, founder or foundational period, scriptures, worldview, worship or practice, growing up in the religion, cultural expressions, calendar and holidays, history, and the religion in the world today.

The books in this series are written by scholars. Their approach to their subject matter is neutral and objective. They are not trying to convert readers to the religion they are describing. Most scholars, however, value the religion they have chosen to study, so you can expect the general tone of these books to be appreciative rather than critical.

Religious studies scholars are experts in their field, but they are not critics in the same sense in which one might be an art, film, or literary critic. Religious studies scholars feel obligated to describe a tradition faithfully and accurately, and to interpret it in a way that will allow nonbelievers as well as believers to grasp its essential structure, but they do not feel compelled to pass judgment on it. Their goal is to increase knowledge and understanding.

Academic writing has a reputation for being dry and uninspiring. If so, religious studies scholarship is an exception. Scholars of religion have the happy task of describing the words and deeds of some of the world's most amazing people: founders, prophets, sages, saints, martyrs, and bodhisattvas.

The power of religion moves us. Today, as in centuries past, people thrill to the ethical vision of Confucianism, or the dancing beauty of Hinduism's images of the divine. They are challenged by the one, holy God of the Jews, and comforted by the saving promise of Christianity. They are inspired by the stark purity of

Islam, by the resilience of tribal religions, by the energy and innovation of the new religions. The religions have retained such a strong hold on so many people's lives over such a long period of time largely because they are unforgettable.

Religious ideas, institutions, and professions are among the oldest in humanity's history. They have outlasted the world's great empires. Their authority and influence have endured far beyond that of Earth's greatest philosophers, military leaders, social engineers, or politicians. It is this that makes them so attractive to those who seek power and influence, whether such people intend to use their power and influence for good or evil. Unfortunately, in the hands of the wrong person, religious ideas might as easily be responsible for the destruction of the world as for its salvation. All that stands between us and that outcome is the knowledge of the general populace. In this as in any other field, people must be able to critically assess what they are being told.

The authors and editors of this series hope that all who seek to wield the tremendous powers of religion will do so with unselfish and noble intent. Knowing how unlikely it is that that will always be the case, we seek to provide the basic knowledge necessary to critically assess the degree to which contemporary religious claims are congruent with the history, scriptures, and genius of the traditions they are supposed to represent.

Ann Marie B. Bahr
South Dakota State University

1

Introduction

All that we are is the result of what we have thought:
it is founded on our thoughts.
If a man speaks or acts with an evil thought,
pain follows him, as the wheel follows
the foot of the ox that draws the carriage.

—The Buddha, "The Twin-Verses"

IMPRESSIONS OF BUDDHISM

What do you think of when you hear the word Buddhism? Do you think of places in Asia, such as China or Japan? Maybe you think of martial arts, such as karate or kung fu. Until very recently, these were the impressions many people in the United States had of Buddhism. However, Buddhism is now becoming better known and different images of Buddhism may come to mind.

Perhaps you have heard of the *Dalai Lama*, the Nobel Peace Prize winner and great advocate for human rights. Maybe you have seen movies that featured Buddhism such as *Kundun* or *Little Buddha*, which starred Keanu Reeves as the *Buddha*. If you have visited a bookstore recently, you may have encountered a section that contained books on Asian thought and marveled at the many books on the shelves. You might even know that some famous people are Buddhists, such as Richard Gere, Steven Seagal, Tina Turner, and members of the music group the Beastie Boys. You may actually know someone or even have a friend who is a Buddhist.

DEMOGRAPHICS AND DISTRIBUTION

Buddhism is considered a "world religion" because it has spread all over the globe. Listed below are the five most populous religions in the United States, by number of devotees, and changes from 1990 to 2000:

RELIGION	2001 EST. POPULATION	PERCENT OF U.S. POP., 2000	PERCENT CHANGE 1990–2000
Christianity	159,030,000	76.5%	+5%
Nonreligious	27,539,000	13.2%	+110%
Judaism	2,831,000	1.3%	-10%
Islam	1,104,000	0.5%	+109%
Buddhism	1,082,000	0.5%	+170%
(Source: adherents.com, ARIS)			

The fact that there are approximately as many Buddhists as Muslims in the United States is surprising to many, and so is the fact that Buddhism is increasing more rapidly as a percentage of the United States' population than any other group listed. The growth in the number of Buddhists has come from two sources: (1) Buddhists who have immigrated to the United States from other countries, and (2) people already residing in the United States who have converted to Buddhism or been raised Buddhist.

The above data underscore the importance of learning about other religious traditions. While Christianity dominates the religious sphere in the United States, the substantial percentage increase of Muslims and Buddhists should encourage us to study these traditions. Some estimates of the number of Buddhists who reside in the United States actually range up to three million, which, if true, would mean that more self-identified Buddhists live in the United States than self-identified Jews!

There are approximately 360 million Buddhists worldwide, making Buddhism the fourth-largest religion in the world after Christianity, Islam, and Hinduism. The countries with the largest per-capita population of Buddhists are all found in Asia:

COUNTRY	PERCENTAGE OF POPULATION THAT IS BUDDHIST
Thailand	95%
Cambodia	90%
Myanmar	88%
Bhutan	75%
Sri Lanka	70%
Tibet	65%*
Laos	60%
Vietnam	55%
Japan	50%*
Macau	45% (below 50 percent but with a substantial population)
Taiwan	43%

(Source: adherents.com. * The accuracy of the data on Tibet and Japan is questionable; this point will be taken up later in the text.)

We have now seen that there are millions of Buddhists in the West and hundreds of millions of Buddhists in the world. The next logical questions might be, "Where did Buddhism begin?" and "When did it arrive in all of these other countries?"

HISTORY OF BUDDHIST EXPANSION ACROSS ASIA
India
Buddhism began in India around 500 B.C.E., where it grew and flourished. The three major types of Buddhism (Theravâda, Mahâyâna, and Vajrayâna) had their beginnings in India. In the third century B.C.E., India's Emperor Aśoka (Ashoka) sent Buddhist missionaries to surrounding areas and countries. The first set of Buddhist scriptures, the Pali Canon, was composed in India. Great monastic universities were built, and scholars from the rest of Asia traveled to India to learn in these universities. Buddhist art and philosophy originated in India. However, after the thirteenth century C.E., Buddhism almost disappeared from India, leaving only small remnant Buddhist communities in the land of its birth.

Sri Lanka
In the middle of the third century B.C.E., Emperor Aśoka sent Buddhist missionaries to Sri Lanka, where the king was converted to Buddhism. By the second century B.C.E., Buddhism had become the dominant religion in Sri Lanka. The form of Buddhism that flourished here is called Theravâda Buddhism. Sri Lanka was a center of Buddhist culture and scholarship in the first centuries of the Common Era. Buddhism never died out in Sri Lanka, as it had in India, but it suffered periods of decline. The most recent of these occurred under Portuguese, Dutch, and British colonial rule. However, a successful movement to revive Buddhism in Sri Lanka began in the latter half of the nineteenth century; this movement bore fruit that is still evident today.

Central Asia
Emperor Aśoka also sent missionaries to the northwest, into

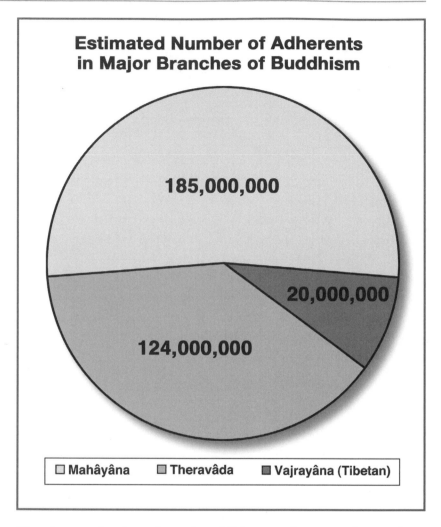

Estimated Number of Adherents in Major Branches of Buddhism

185,000,000

20,000,000

124,000,000

☐ Mahâyâna   ☐ Theravâda   ■ Vajrayâna (Tibetan)

The three major branches of Buddhism—Mahâyâna, Theravâda, and Vajrayâna—all originated in India. Today, the largest branch is Mahâyâna Buddhism, with 185,000,000 adherents worldwide.

present-day Pakistan and Afghanistan. This region, which straddled the ancient trade routes, became another center of Buddhist learning. Two giant Buddha statues were carved out of a mountain in Afghanistan between the second and the fifth centuries C.E., and destroyed by the Taliban in February–March 2001. The Buddhists had left the area by the fifteenth century, but long before that occurred the Chinese were exposed for the first time to Buddhism as they traveled along these central Asian trade routes.

China

The Han dynasty extended its power into Central Asia in the first century B.C.E., and the Chinese people learned about Buddhism, most likely from the monks dwelling in the cave monasteries located along the trade routes. A community of Chinese Buddhists existed by the middle of the first century C.E. The first major task of Chinese Buddhism was the translation of texts from Indian languages into Chinese. As Buddhism grew in importance, a number of different schools developed. After a persecution by a Taoist emperor in the middle of the ninth century, the different schools of Buddhism were combined, and this combined form of Buddhism has continued to the present day in China.

Korea

A Chinese monk introduced Korea to Buddhism in the second half of the fourth century C.E. Shortly after, a monk from Central Asia arrived in a different part of what is today Korea, but the Central Asian influence quickly died out. Korean Buddhism derived from Chinese Buddhism; many Korean monks traveled to China to study. Buddhism enjoyed royal support in Korea until the fourteenth century. From the end of the fourteenth century to the beginning of the twentieth century, Confucianism was the only official religion in Korea. Buddhism was forcibly suppressed during this period, but it clung to life. Following the Japanese annexation (1910) and subsequent occupation of Korea, Buddhism was allowed to grow, and the revival has continued to the present time. Today, Buddhism is once again an important influence in Korea.

Japan

In the sixth century C.E., Buddhism was introduced to Japan by a Korean king, who sent images of the Buddha and Buddhist texts as a way of establishing peaceful relations between the two kingdoms. Prince Shotoku, a devout Buddhist who extended royal patronage to the religion, did much to promote Buddhism's growth in the early seventh century. During his reign, monks were sent to China to study Buddhism. Beginning in the Nara period (eighth century), Chinese monks brought many Chinese Buddhist schools to Japan. Japanese monks continued to enjoy royal patronage, and they served in administrative positions and performed other government roles. When political power was transferred to the samurai warriors at the close of the twelfth century, Buddhism continued to be treated favorably by the new rulers for several centuries. During this period, distinctly Japanese forms of Buddhism arose. From the sixteenth to the nineteenth century, Buddhism fell out of favor with the military rulers. In the twentieth century, many new religious movements developed out of the older forms of Buddhism. The older forms continued to grow and develop alongside the newer forms of Buddhism.

Southeast Asia: Myanmar/Burma, Thailand, Cambodia, Laos, Vietnam, Indonesia, and Malaysia

By the early centuries of the Common Era, both Hindu and Buddhist merchants from India had established trading stations in Southeast Asia. Various forms of Indian Buddhism were established in these countries. Sometimes there was also an infusion of Chinese forms of Buddhism. The type of Buddhism that eventually came to dominate in each of these countries is listed below:

Myanmar/Burma	Theravâda
Thailand	Theravâda
Cambodia	Theravâda
Laos	Theravâda
Vietnam	Mahâyâna
Malaysia and Indonesia	Mahâyâna

As you can see, Theravâda Buddhism is the most prevalent form of Buddhism in Southeast Asia. With the exception of Sri Lanka, this form of Buddhism does not dominate in any Asian country outside of Southeast Asia.

Tibet

Tibet lay beyond the main trade routes between China and present-day Afghanistan. Even though Buddhists lived in other places in Central Asia by the beginning of the Common Era, Buddhism did not enter Tibet until much later. King Srong-tsan-gam-po united the warring Tibetan clans for the first time in the seventh century. His two wives, one from China and the other from Nepal, were both Buddhists. Before long, the king had adopted the faith. Tibet's Buddhism developed through contact with India. Tibetan kings invited famous Indian scholars and meditation masters to come to Tibet. After Buddhism faded in India, Tibetan Buddhism kept many Indian traditions alive, and used them to develop its own unique form of Buddhism. In the sixteenth century, the institution of the Dalai Lama was officially recognized for the first time. In the middle of the twentieth century, Tibet came under the control of the Communist leaders of the People's Republic of China, and Buddhism was suppressed.

By the seventh century c.e., Buddhism had spread across Asia. It had subdivided into various schools and made its home among numerous nationalities. Is there anything that all these people who practiced Buddhism had in common? What distinguishes a Buddhist from a non-Buddhist? Or, in other words, who is a Buddhist?

WHO IS A BUDDHIST?

What makes a person a Buddhist? While this book will try to answer this question in more detail over the course of its pages, it is useful to offer a short definition. A Buddhist is a person who believes in the major tenets of Buddhist thought as articulated by the respective traditions of the school of Buddhism that the believer follows.

What are the major tenets of Buddhism? All Buddhists look to Gautama Buddha as the founder of their religion. Importantly, Buddhists do *not* claim that the Buddha was a god but only a human being. This view will be made more complex when we briefly examine Buddhist history and learn that most Buddhists are devotional (they worship a deity). Nonetheless, Buddhists view the founder of their religion as a human rather than a god.

As we will learn, there is not a single sacred book in Buddhism that would offer an exact parallel to the Jewish Bible, the Christian Bible, or the Qur'an of Islam. There is a textual tradition in Buddhism, but Buddhists differ on the importance of one book or *sutra* over another. Some schools assert that one sutra is more complete than others, while others are adherents of a series of texts, and still others argue for not following any texts.

Buddhists follow an ethical code that includes many of the same ethical priorities found in other religious traditions: do not murder, lie, steal, etc. Buddhists apply their ethical code to their words as well as their deeds. They believe in acting in ways that are consistent with benevolence and love. A Buddhist views another person as identical with her or his own self and thus attempts to treat people and other sentient (conscious) life with high regard. Correspondingly, many Buddhists may not engage in such activities as hunting, military service, or eating meat; however, this is not true for all Buddhists.

Buddhists, with some notable exceptions, are not aggressive proselytizers. While they do believe that Buddhism is the correct path, and they furthermore believe that it is an act of compassion to acquaint others with the *dharma* (Buddhist truth or Buddhist teaching), they also acknowledge that some people may not be ready to pursue the path at this point in their lives, at least not exclusively. In religious studies, we sometimes speak of the three "missionary" traditions of Christianity, Islam, and Buddhism—all three have intentionally spread throughout the world. Yet, of these three, the global migration of Buddhism has not been as exclusivist or extensive (or, for that matter, as bloody) as has the spread of Islam or Christianity. That is not to say, as is sometimes suggested, that Buddhist history is without its violent episodes and periods of oppression. As with Islam and Christianity, it is a religion that promotes both peace and traditions of peace, but it has fallen short of its authentic message at times.

Most Buddhists are devotional Buddhists: They pray or chant to a deity similar to the way in which a Christian, Jew, Muslim,

LOVE IN BUDDHISM AND CHRISTIANITY

Love is an important term in every religion in the world. The Christian theologian, Paul Tillich, regards love as the "drive towards the reunion of the separated." Tillich considers the criterion and corrective of every act of love to be the distinctively Christ-like love called *agapê*. Agapê is God's love for humans in spite of their unworthiness. While the love between God and the human person can be a very close relationship, even to the extent of Christ being "in" the believer and the believer being "in" Christ, the distinction between the believer and either God or Christ remains. In this kind of love, the "reunion of the separated" is a participatory love, with the one participating in the life of the other. It is not, however, a non-dual love because the distinction between the divine and the human person remains.

Using Tillich's definition, the Buddhist experience of Awakening might be described as "Fulfilled Love" because in it the separated are reunited through the realization that there is no other apart from oneself. Or, in other words, love arises at the same time as one realizes the non-dual nature of the Universe. In Awakening to Fulfilled Love, all obstacles to love are, at last and evermore, overcome.

Love in Buddhism is not simply self-denial for the sake of the other, for as long as there is a "self" to be denied and an "other" to be served, one is still living in duality. As long as there is duality (self and other), the taint of self-interest (*hubris*) can be mitigated but not extirpated. Buddhism proposes that genuine love transcends all dualities and retains no vestige of self-interest.

One might say that as agapê is love "in spite of [our unworthiness]," Buddhist love is love "just because of [our identity, our non-duality]." While the theistic traditions focus on a participatory love, Buddhism proposes what we might call an identity-participatory love because it includes both the lover and loved in a dynamic, synergistic at-one-ment.

or Hindu might. While meditation is an important Buddhist practice, not as many Buddhists actually meditate as the stereotypical portrayal of Buddhism would suggest.

The Buddhist place of worship is called a temple. In addition to attending worship services, Buddhists will also visit the temple for special occasions, such as weddings, funerals, or festivals, and for special blessings. Many Buddhists also practice at home. They have small altars in their residence, which serve as the focal point for their prayers or other rituals.

In terms of its social structure, Buddhism is more like Catholic or Orthodox Christianity than it is like Protestant Christianity. Buddhism has monks and nuns, that is, it divides the Buddhist community up into monks, nuns, and laypeople. In Theravâda Buddhism,[1] *sangha* refers only to those who have chosen a monastic lifestyle. In Mahâyâna Buddhism, sangha often means the entire Buddhist community, including monks, nuns, and laypeople. Buddhist monks and nuns frequently live in temples and are financially supported by the laypersons. The laypersons, usually called "householders" in Buddhist literature, gain merit for this good deed, and receive services from the monastery (e.g., sermons, performance of rituals) in return for their economic support. Buddhist temples can vary widely in scale and design—from simple houses to elaborate multiacre properties with many subtemples contained within the walls that enclose the perimeter of the property.

In sum, many of the ethical precepts and even much of the social structure of Buddhism is very similar to what one might find in other religious traditions, even Western traditions. When we turn to consider the worldview of Buddhism, we will find less similarity with Western religions (although some remains) and more similarity with Hinduism. Hinduism and Buddhism both participated in the ancient South Asian worldview. (The two religions eventually separated geographically and, as they did so, their worldviews correspondingly diverged.) Ancient Buddhism was different from ancient Hinduism exactly to the extent that the Buddha's teachings differed from the teaching of his Hindu contemporaries. In other words, what distinguished the first Buddhists was that they were disciples of the Buddha. And what, exactly, were or are the teachings of the Buddha? The answer to that question depends on which subgroup of Buddhists you are asking, and therefore a full explanation will have to wait until a later chapter. At this point, however, I will touch briefly on a few teachings that apply to all Buddhists.

KARMA AND REBIRTH

Perhaps one of the most common ideas that people in the West associate with Buddhism is *karma*. Buddhists do believe in karma, but they are not the only ones. All the major religions born in the South Asian cultural realm—not only Buddhism but also Hinduism, Jainism, and Sikhism—share the doctrine of karma.

Since the word has entered Western vocabulary, you may already have some idea of what karma means. Karma is the principle of return: What you give you receive back. So, if I kick a dog this morning and in the afternoon that dog bites me (or maybe some other misfortune besets me), that is karma playing itself out. Contrary to this example, the action that led to the result is usually unknown, but Buddhists will still say, "It is his good [or bad] karma that has brought this on," when something either positive or negative happens to a person.

Karma literally means "action," but it is action as accompanied by the consequences of the action for the doer of the action. Buddhism is primarily concerned with the moral character of actions. In every action, there is a moral element that determines whether it is a good or bad deed. That moral element is determined not by the results but by the motive of the action. If you intend to do good but your action has bad results (e.g., if you hold a door for someone to walk through and they inadvertently trip and break an ankle), your karmic accumulation for that deed is good not bad.

The doctrine of karma provides a sense that we live in a world where justice is done, where bad deeds are punished, and good deeds are rewarded. In retributive fashion, karma is at work. Some people also like the idea of karma because it suggests that there is a reason for everything that happens—the universe is not chaotic but logical. Others may be attracted to karma because judgment isn't necessarily handed down at death but rather during one's life.

However, if we take karma without the idea of rebirth, then we really don't have an accurate picture. According to Buddhist thought, rebirth is the lot of all humans.[2] We have all lived many lives before, and we will live many lives in the future until we gain release from this cycle of birth-death-rebirth (*samsara*) through Awakening.

What determines the conditions in which we will live our next life is the karma we have accrued over this and previous lifetimes. For a Buddhist, then, the idea is to do as much good as one can from right intentions, thereby accumulating good karma, which will result in a favorable rebirth. And, hopefully, one of these rebirths will be such that it will result in the state of Awakening after which no karma will be accumulated and therefore no subsequent rebirth experienced.

Allow me to underline that last point: Continuous rebirth is not desirable in Buddhism. The goal is to escape from this cycle. This is different from how Westerners sometimes perceive reincarnation. They like the idea of multiple births and deaths, but this is not a Buddhist attitude.

After hearing an explanation of karma-rebirth, people frequently ask, "If people are continuously reborn, how do we account for the number of people who are currently alive as opposed to those who existed before? If there are no new souls who enter the universe, then how can Buddhism account for the increase in the world's population?"

The question may be answered several ways (including the answer that it truly doesn't benefit the Buddhist practitioner to be concerned with this problem), but the most common answer appeals to the idea of *lokas*. Lokas are other levels of sentient existence (deities, animals, hungry ghosts, etc.). A being can enter the human realm from any other loka. Human life is the preferred form of existence; only a human can reach Awakening and be released from continued rebirth. Yet, although Buddhism does proffer an answer to this question—one that may help to make numerical sense of the doctrine—in the end the Buddhist simply takes it on faith that the doctrine of karma-rebirth is operative in his or her life and that this will be confirmed at the moment of Awakening.

THE BUDDHIST IDEA OF AWAKENING

The idea of "Awakening" is another essential aspect of Buddhism. It was previously noted that Awakening is the goal of Buddhism and that it marks the end of the karma-rebirth cycle.

As you read how various Buddhists define this term, you may associate it with beliefs from other religious traditions, and appropriately so, as one could argue that the Hindu idea of moksha, the Taoist idea of realizing the Tao, or even the descriptions of Christian, Muslim, or Jewish mystics seem similar. So, while arguably the Buddhist endpoint or solution to life's dilemmas may not be unique to Buddhism, it is an essential part of Buddhist belief.

The Buddhist Awakening is often referred to by different terms, including *nirvana*, enlightenment, and *satori*. As with the term karma, nirvana has come to be widely used in American popular culture. There was, of course, a famous rock band of that name, but you also find the term used in newspapers and popular magazines to connote something that is mystical or a peak experience (a "nirvana-like experience"). (The Japanese Buddhist term *Zen* is used in almost the same fashion and with a similar meaning in popular publications.) Nirvana is defined in a dictionary as follows:

> 1) *Hinduism* a blowing out, or extinction, of the flame of life through reunion with the Brahma 2) *Buddhism* the state of perfect blessedness achieved by the extinction of individual existence and by the absorption of the soul into the supreme

spirit, or by the extinction of all desires and passions 3) any place or condition of great peace or bliss.[3]

The third definition is the one that likely applies to the popular usage of the term nirvana. The definition ascribed to Buddhism (#2) is actually a conflation of Hindu and Buddhist ideas. Two of the terms, namely the "soul" and the "supreme spirit," find no place in Buddhism, although they would be acceptable translations for the Hindu concepts of the Atman and the Brahman, respectively. So, the first thing we can learn from this definition is the importance of seeking expert advice and double-checking the accuracy of anything you read about Buddhism! However, the remainder of the definition ("the state of perfect blessedness achieved by the extinction of individual existence . . . or by the extinction of all desires and passions") does provide an adequate provisional idea of what nirvana actually means for a Buddhist.

All Buddhists strive to reach nirvana, if not in this life, then in their next life. Buddhism differs from those religions that place the resolution of life's drama postmortem; it insists that nirvana can be attained prior to death. However, nirvana can only be attained by a human being. It cannot be attained from either a subhuman or a superhuman realm of existence. Buddhism strongly encourages believers to strive for nirvana in this very lifetime. After all, due to the effects of karma-rebirth, one may not be born human in the next life or, even if born human, one may not come to encounter Buddhist thought at all.

Though all Buddhists strive to reach nirvana, they do so in different ways. Some forms of Buddhism teach that only monks can hope to attain nirvana. Laypersons try to accumulate as much positive karma as possible in this life in anticipation of a next life where they may be better placed to pursue monastic practice. Other Buddhists believe that it is through devotion to a Buddha that one can be delivered at death into a "pure land" of Awakening (this will be elaborated on later in the text). Still other forms of Buddhism teach that even laypersons who work diligently at it may experience Awakening prior to death.

What is the actual experience of Awakening? This will require a detailed explanation, but for now we can say that Awakening is not the same as understanding. That is, I can read and intellectually understand Buddhist thought, but this is not what is meant by Awakening. Awakening is an actualization, a realization of the authentic nature of existence, including one's own existence. Without experiencing Awakening, the person remains in ignorance (*avidya*) and suffering (*dukkha*).

Let's turn now to the life story of the Buddha and his first teaching. In the discussion of his first teaching, we will better come to understand why Buddhists believe that we are currently living an inauthentic existence, as well as why they believe that Awakening is the ultimate answer for all human beings.

2

Foundations

*The story of the Buddha's personal life . . . is the
story of someone who attained full enlightenment
through hard work and unwavering dedication.*

—Tenzin Gyatso, His Holiness,
the Fourteenth Dalai Lama,
in *The World of Tibetan Buddhism*

The name of the founder of Buddhism was not, as many people think, Buddha. "Buddha" is a title, not a proper name. It means "the Awakened One." As we look at the biography of the Buddha, it is important to remember that there are disagreements about the particulars of his birth, life, and death, and there are legendary elements entwined with historical memories. Although the Buddha's story was lovingly and faithfully transmitted from generation to generation, the concern of the storytellers was not historical accuracy but rather the importance of his life as a model for Buddhist life. In this chapter, I will follow the lead of those ancient storytellers and seek to answer this question: What was it about the Buddha's life that enabled an entire religion to be built upon his experiences?

THE BUDDHA'S EARLY LIFE

According to the story, the Buddha was born in Lumbinî, in what is now Nepal. The most commonly conjectured year of his birth is 563 B.C.E. His family name was Gautama, and his given name was Siddhartha, which means "he who has achieved his goal."[4] He was also called Sâkyamuni, meaning "sage of the Sâkyas" (his father's clan and therefore his clan). His ancestral home was Kapilavastu, a nearby town.

Siddhartha was born into a royal family (his father was a local chieftain) and grew up as a prince. His birth was miraculous. His mother, Queen Mâyâ, gave birth to Siddhartha while standing up and holding to a branch of a tree. It was not a normal birth; instead, the infant emerged, painlessly, from his mother's side. Interestingly, as author John Strong notes in his excellent account, *The Buddha: A Short Biography*, "This lack of passing through the birth canal is often said to reflect a concern for purity, but it may also be connected to a pan-Indian tradition that asserts that the trauma of vaginal birth is what wipes out the memory of previous lives."[5] Strong's point is important because, according to the doctrine of transmigration or rebirth, Siddhartha would have experienced multiple births prior to the one in which he became the Buddha. The Buddhist tradition recounts some of these previous lives in texts called *Jâtakas* ("birth stories"). Siddhartha was subsequently able to recall all of his previous lives as a result of attaining the Awakening experience. A week after giving birth to Siddhartha, Queen Mâyâ died and the king married her sister, Prajâpatî.

The accounts of Siddhartha's birth include indications of his coming auspiciousness. Some accounts say that he immediately stood up and walked and talked, declaring that this would be his last birth, and that he would bring others to liberation. Siddhartha's father, King Suddhodana, had several holy men predict his son's future through a process called divination. In examining the child's body, they found thirty-two physical manifestations that indicated the infant would grow up to be either a great king or a great spiritual leader and teacher. Suddhodana wanted his son to succeed him on the throne.

Determined that Siddhartha should become a great king, Suddhodana surrounded his son with the pleasures of life, hoping thereby to deter him from developing any interest in religion. In this way, Siddhartha grew up to become a young man, married a princess named Yaśodharâ, and had a son named Râhula (which means "to fetter," perhaps indicating that Siddhartha felt confined). It seemed that Suddhodana had successfully steered his son toward kingship and away from religious life.

However, it was not to be. Siddhartha lived a very sheltered life, secluded in a castle and showered with all of life's luxuries. He eventually grew bored and wanted to travel beyond the castle walls to a beautiful park he had heard about. His father granted him this wish but had his subjects prepare the road that Siddhartha's chariot would take so that there would be no distractions. At twenty-nine years of age, the prince stepped into his chariot with his charioteer and embarked on a trip that would change the world forever.

As Prince Siddhartha was traveling on the road, he encountered an old man who piqued his interest. Due to his father's protection, he had never seen a person slowed by extreme age. Siddhartha asked Chandaka, his charioteer, to explain the man's condition. Chandaka replied, "Old age, it is called, the destroyer of beauty and vigor, the source of sorrow, the depriver of pleasures, the slayer of memories, the enemy of sense organs. This man has been ruined by old age. He too in his infancy has taken milk and, in due time, had crawled on the ground; he then became a handsome youth, and now he has reached old age."[6]

Siddhartha very naturally then asked whether this condition is unique to this person or if all humans grow old. Chandaka retorted, "Advanced age will certainly come upon you through the inescapable force of time, no matter how long you may live. People in the world are aware of old age, yet they seek [pleasures]."[7]

The prince, learning that he too would grow old, was shaken, and decided to forego the anticipated pleasantness of the park and return at once to the protection of the castle. The castle did provide physical protection for the prince but his mind was no longer protected, and he began to think deeply about the idea of aging, which troubled his thoughts. But he shared his unease with no one.

Soon he decided to travel once again from the castle and asked his father for permission to visit the park he failed to reach. The king, unaware of any consternation in his son, granted his wish and prepared the road as before to be free of distraction or disturbance.

Again, the prince set out in his chariot for the park and, again, the path provided a lesson as the prince this time came upon a novel sight: a man who appeared very ill. As he had with the old man, Siddhartha queried his driver about the situation and learned that the man was sick. Siddhartha asked if he too might suffer a similar fate at some point in his life. The charioteer assured the prince that he would at some time fall prey to sickness saying, "Prince, this evil is common to all; yet the world filled with suffering seeks enjoyment, however oppressed it is by disease."[8]

The prince became agitated and fled back to the castle fraught with concern over his inevitable fate. Siddhartha did not know where to turn. What had been a sheltered world was turned upside down, and the corporeal pleasures of food, fine clothes, and viewing dancing girls were becoming pointless. He reasoned, "If one inevitably falls prey to sickness and age, what is the point in the pleasures of the day?"

A third trip eventually followed in which Siddhartha witnessed the most sobering sight of all: a funeral where he saw the body of a dead man. "This is the last state of all men. Death is certain for all; whether they be of low, middle, or high degree," [9] averred his charioteer.

This sight shook the prince to his very core and robbed him, once and for all, of satisfaction with his life of privilege and position. He could no longer stand to live and returned to the palace to contemplate his ultimate fate.

Fortunately, he encountered a fourth sight. He saw a holy man, a Hindu saddhu. This encounter, though, was different: It did not represent a problem for Siddhartha but a solution. The holy man seemed to have found peace despite the sickness, old age, and death that awaited him. The saddhu told Siddhartha, "In this world which is characterized by destruction, I eagerly search for the blessed and indestructible state." [10] Hearing this, Siddhartha knew what he had to do . . . and he conspired to leave the only world he had ever known and seek the truth of his human existence.

One night, after furtively kissing his wife and son good-bye, he snuck away into the woods and took up the life of a wandering holy man, just like the one he had encountered.

In Buddhism, the four events Siddhartha witnessed—sick man, old man, dead man, and the holy man—are referred to as the Four Passing Sights. "The Great Renunciation" refers to the night when Siddhartha fled the palace to begin his new life.

Siddhartha spent the next few years studying and practicing with the most esteemed Hindu holy men of his time. In Hinduism, someone who renounces the world to spend all his time seeking truth is called a sannyasin. The sannyasin, or world-renouncer, removes himself from life to devote all his efforts to freeing himself from the bonds of karma and attaining the deathless state. [11]

Yet, despite or perhaps because of these efforts, Siddhartha still felt that the basic problem of human existence was not answered to his satisfaction. This part of his story serves to illustrate Siddhartha's great determination, and also to show that Hinduism did not provide the answer he sought. He had to traverse a new path.

In desperation, he took a severely ascetic[12] approach, which meant he practiced extreme breath control and lived on small amounts of water and food. These were time-honored yogic practices employed by ascetics at that time. They were used to generate certain mental and spiritual states. Siddhartha subjected himself to a fast so severe that he became emaciated and almost died. While Siddhartha was not impressed with the results of this course of action, others admired his strong will and ascetic proficiency. He became the recognized leader of a small band of five ascetics.

When he found himself at the brink of death from starvation, Siddhartha realized that the life of deprivation was no more valid than the life of excess that he had enjoyed as a prince. Surely, he thought, a middle way was best. He decided to eat again, beginning with an offering of milk-rice from a passing local woman named Sujâtâ, and his health was soon restored. One of the consequences of his abandonment of extreme asceticism in favor of the "middle way" was that his five ascetic companions became alienated and then left him in disgust. (According to Buddhist tradition, these five ascetics would subsequently return to listen to the Buddha's first sermon and become his first disciples.)

Siddhartha then took a fateful step: He sat down under a fig tree with the firm intent of not moving until he had realized authentic truth. "My body may shrivel up, my skin, my bones, my flesh may dissolve, but [I] will not move from this very seat until I have obtained enlightenment."[13]

Settling himself under the tree, he meditated and waited. Over the course of a momentous night, he withstood the attempts of *Mâra*, the Great Tempter, to dissuade him from his mission.

Mâra was a liar and a deceiver, a sort of Buddhist version of the devil. He tried to distract Siddhartha by parading voluptuous goddesses before him, by pelting him with fiery missiles, and by impugning his moral right to pursue Awakening rather than fulfilling his roles in society. Siddhartha steadfastly continued to meditate. At last, as dawn broke, Siddhartha experienced Awakening. He is said to have gained knowledges, both mundane and divine.

The knowledge Siddhartha gained as part of his Awakening included supernormal powers (he was able to hear all sounds and could recall all of his former lives) as well as the foundational dharma or truth of Buddhism.[14] His search had taken six

THE BUDDHA'S SECOND SERMON

Studies of Buddhism usually emphasize the Buddha's First Sermon after his Awakening as it is said to encapsulate the primary teaching of Buddhism. There is some truth to the claim, but the Buddha's second sermon, preached at Benares (in modern-day northern India), is also worthy of special consideration.

In his second sermon, the Buddha connected his discourse on the nature of suffering to two other important doctrines: non-self (anâtman) and impermanence (anitya). Along with dukkha, these three comprise what are called the Three Marks of Existence.

Non-self is a challenging concept, even for someone who has studied Buddhism for many years. The idea is not that one has no self or that one does not exist, as Westerners often understood it when they first learned of this doctrine. It is rather that this ordinary self, this collection of physical and mental aggregates, is impermanent, relative, and nonexistent in and of itself. One suffers or is unsatisfied because of a failure to fully realize this limited nature of the self. We do not know that this is the reason for our suffering, however, and therefore we look outside the self for answers to our problems.

Zen Buddhism speaks of the realization of the True Self. The True Self sees the nondual nature of the Self as naturally as he or she previously viewed the inauthentic self. The True Self is grounded in a permanent, absolute, and ever-existing reality. It was as a result of this teaching, and by profoundly experiencing this truth, that the five ascetics that the Buddha was teaching attained Awakening.

full years; he was thirty-five years old when he at last became a Buddha (an Awakened One).

LIFE AS THE BUDDHA AND *PARINIRVÂṆÂ*

Siddhartha began to teach, and to attract followers, beginning with the five ascetic companions who had left him. His teaching career lasted approximately forty-five years. The Buddha's converts included mainly members of the lower classes but also some Brahmins and Kshatriyas, and also many members of his own family. (Brahmins and Kshatriyas were members of the highest social classes, including priests, teachers, rulers, and warriors.)

Why was the Buddha able to attract so many followers? One reason was that Buddhism was a religion that intentionally tried to spread its message. The sixth and fifth centuries B.C.E. were a period of religious ferment in ancient India; many people were looking for spiritual solutions to life's problems. Some holy men waited for seekers to come to them and beg to be taught their wisdom, while others used their homeless state as an opportunity to travel and preach their message. The Buddha was one of the latter—he and his band of monks traveled the roads of India, preaching and teaching. Buddhism later became, along with Islam and Christianity, one of the world's three large missionary religions.

Another reason for the popularity of the new religion was Buddhism's relatively progressive social attitude. Buddhism offered women an independent spiritual path, one in which they were not dependent on their husbands or fathers. (We will discuss the addition of women to the sangha later in the text.) Buddhism accepted the second son in a family, even though second sons were not usually included in the inheritance, and therefore did not bring any wealth into the sangha. It even accepted the so-called outcastes, the poorest of India's poor.

Perhaps a third reason for Buddhism's popularity was that it retained some of the essential teachings of Hinduism (karma and rebirth), and it had a "guru" (spiritual teacher) in the person of the Buddha. In other words, there was some common ground between the two faiths, making conversion from Hinduism to Buddhism less dramatic and traumatic than conversion to a Western religion. Finally, the strength of the Buddha's message and the fact that he was a charismatic teacher also contributed to the rapid spread of Buddhism.

Prior to his death, the Buddha and his closest disciple and cousin, Ânanda, traveled throughout India delivering messages that focused on the continued existence of the sangha after the Buddha's death. Although he was eighty years old and ill, the Buddha was still able—due to his strength of mind—to forestall death and continue to impart dharma (the Buddhist teaching).

He traveled to Pâpâ, a small town where he was provided a meal by Cunda, a devotee and a blacksmith by trade. The traditional accounts of this meal and its resulting effects upon the Buddha are inconclusive, but it is often conjectured that he ate tainted food, which contributed to his death, though it is quite likely that the Buddha was near death prior to the visit. Some sources have suggested the meal contained pork, others mushrooms or other foods. The Buddha did praise the food and Cunda was able to receive only positive karmic benefit from feeding the Buddha and his party.

The Buddha finally returned to the outskirts of Kuśinagarî, which was to be the site of his *parinirvâṇâ*. He lay down on his side in what has become known as the position of parinirvâṇâ. Others assembled around him and various encounters ensued, but the time finally arrived for his death. He then uttered his final words: "Now monks, I declare to you: all conditioned things are of a nature to decay—strive on untiringly." [15]

The Buddha is said to have passed into parinirvâṇâ, the state beyond Awakening. He was therefore released from the cycle of birth and rebirth (samsara). At the Buddha's departure, an earthquake occured. The monks and others near to him mourned his death and preparations followed for handling his body and cremation. As in Hinduism, the Buddhist tradition is to cremate the body rather than to bury it.

GAUTAMA'S FIRST TEACHING:
THE FOUR NOBLE TRUTHS

Upon finally achieving Awakening, the question Siddhartha was required to answer was, "What am I to do with this wisdom, this *bodhi*?" His initial thought was to keep this knowledge to himself, fearing misunderstanding and negative reprisals, but he ultimately decided that he should tell others of this experience and help them realize the same reality. After all, not only wisdom but compassion as well was at the heart of the Buddha's Awakening experience.

The Buddha then traveled to Sarnath, where he found his five former ascetic companions, and expounded the first teaching of Buddhism before them. This incident is sometimes called the Sermon at Deer Park. This first teaching is critical to an understanding of Buddhism because it describes the fundamental tenets of the religion. Every Buddhist believes in the Four Noble Truths, which is the name given to the content of the Buddha's first sermon.

The first Noble Truth taught that human life is suffering (dukkha). The second Truth is that this suffering is caused by craving or desire (tanha). The third is that this craving or desire can be made to cease. And the fourth is the Eightfold Path, the way to make the craving cease. A way to explain these four Truths is that the first is the nature of human existence, the second the problem with human existence, the third the answer to the problem, and the fourth the way to solve the problem. Since the Four Noble Truths are the core of Buddhist teaching, understanding them will make the rest of our study of Buddhism easier.

The First Noble Truth

Since Buddhist teaching begins with the statement that life is suffering, some people immediately conclude that Buddhists are pessimistic, that is, negative in their outlook. Not being interested in anything negative, they may end up dismissing Buddhism. However, it is important to remember that many of the world's religions would agree that there is something radically wrong with the world, though they have a different term for it: original sin, ignorance, selfishness, impurity, etc. These religions would further agree that the radical wrong in the world is responsible for the sufferings we endure: Original sin leads to death—ignorance to going 'round and 'round in the world as it is, rather than finding and grasping salvation, selfishness to alienation from other people, impurity to alienation from the sacred, and so forth. Religious thought points out the radical wrong and offers a way to avoid the suffering it entails. Buddhist doctrine states the same thing: Human life without realizing the Buddhist answer is a life of suffering.

However, is life really suffering? We usually say that if something isn't broken, don't fix it. Sure, there is unpleasantness in life but generally I am not in pain, hungry, or thirsty. Actually, I am much better off than most people! Why should I complain and see my life as suffering? A Buddhist may answer that this is true for you. You may be a fortunate person who, for the most part, is able to minimize or forestall suffering in your life. However, Buddhism would go on to suggest that your peaceful life might not be absent of suffering after all.

For one thing, as Prince Gautama realized, sickness, old age, and death lie in wait for all of us and all those we know. Though one may enjoy youth, wellness, and life for now, this will not last. Sickness or death may be only minutes away, rather than, as we like to think, in some distant future.

Another way to think about dukkha is to translate it, not as suffering but as dissatisfaction. In this case, the First Noble Truth states that life is unsatisfactory. We tend to live our lives from peak experience to peak experience, almost biding time in between. When an eagerly anticipated experience actually occurs, it often seems not to live up to its advance billing. Almost immediately after attaining what you desired, you begin to wonder what the excitement was about. Then, almost by impulse, you begin to look forward to another event or thing. From a Buddhist perspective, it is the nature of ordinary human consciousness that we tend to never be satisfied with what we have. We seemingly always want something more or different, which leads us to the Second Noble Truth: Suffering is caused by craving.

The Second Noble Truth

The doctrine of dependent co-arising (*pratîtya-samutpâda*) illustrates how the relationship between craving (tanha) and suffering (dukkha) works in human life. Briefly stated, samsara is characterized by a cause-and-effect cycle perpetuated by ordinary consciousness. Trapped in this cycle of births and deaths, we travel from life to life, always craving, always suffering. Each time we are born, we are born in ignorance of the true reality that is illuminated only by Awakening. The unawakened consciousness works in ignorance (avidya) and therefore it generates karma. This generation of karma results in a continuation of ordinary, samsaric consciousness, both in this life and the next. So, we are born in ignorance and generate karma because we are ignorant, and this karma then leads to a new birth in ignorance. It is a perpetual cycle; for as long as the self continues to exist it moves around this circle from birth to death to birth again.

What is ordinary consciousness? It is samsara. It is consciousness that perceives objects, good or bad feelings, and the self. The self is the subject; the self is "I"—not the "I" made into an objective, visible self (as when I look in a mirror, or describe myself), but the subjective "I," the "I" that sees everything else but cannot see itself because the subject-I (as versus the object-I) is invisible. The subject-I is not what is seen but what sees; it is not what is spoken about, but what speaks; not the action but the actor. Invisible, not able to be described because it is not an object, this "I" is nonetheless assumed as the center of all perception, expression, or action. Without it, nothing is seen, said, or done.

In addition to the self, objects are another part of ordinary consciousness. The two poles of ordinary consciousness are the subject-I and objects. We see everything as an object, even though we presume that other persons are subjects just as the "I" is a subject. What is the source of the objects that we perceive in the world? Buddhists believe that the source of these objects is the mind. The world is a seamless whole, but in order to understand the world we need to break it down into smaller parts, parts that we can name and manipulate. We fragment the world into objects for our conscious apprehension.

The third element of ordinary consciousness (in addition to the subject-I and objects) is the feelings that are generated as we come in contact with objects. In apprehending objects, we utilize our senses, and our senses rely on our body and consciousness to function. This functional, sensory engagement with the world inexorably brings feelings into our consciousness, which are distinguished as good or bad feelings, desirable or undesirable. We seek to attain the objects that we view as good or desirable, and we seek to avoid the objects that we consider bad or undesirable. This craving or grasping after those objects that we deem desirable does NOT lead to relief from suffering or dissatisfaction (although we think it will). Rather than release us from the fundamental ignorance from which we began, it simply leads us to a death that results in a rebirth that only lands us back in a new cycle of ignorance. Release from the round of births and deaths requires a fundamental change in consciousness (Awakening), whereas craving is only ordinary consciousness. So craving only lands us back in suffering.

This is a difficult concept, so let's back up and have another go at the Second Noble Truth from another direction. In the second noble truth, the assertion is made that our suffering or dissatisfaction is caused because we crave or desire. In our discussion of the First Noble Truth, it was pointed out that we never seem to reach an end in our desires. We wish for a new car, a date with that handsome boy or beautiful girl, or perhaps even for spiritual gain. Buddhism argues that this is the basic human problem: We are egocentric human beings who strive to feel satisfied but are ultimately unable to achieve fulfillment, and this results in pain and anxiety.

is   Buddhism

ke a look

around you. What do you see? Perhaps you see a desk, another person, a pencil, and certainly you see this book in front of you. In ordinary speech, we call these things objects. There are many objects around you that you can see, touch, taste, smell, or hear. To engage these objects, you have to have an objectifier. That is, you have to have a person who sees these things as objects. A pencil is not a "pencil" until someone sees it as an object that has that meaning for the objectifier. So, in order to have an object, you need a subject (the objectifier). In seeing the pencil, this book, or any object, you are necessarily involved as the objectifier. You are not an object—but a subject—so we can call you the subject-I.

Normally human consciousness posits a self, that is, it includes self-consciousness. Just because my consciousness functions the way it does, I believe I have a self, even though I can never see the self directly. Consciousness works by using a subject-object polarity, and the self is consciousness' subject. With the self occupying the role of the subject, everything else, including other persons, becomes an object.[16] This subject-object view of the world is our ordinary way of seeing and being in the world and so it is not considered unusual or strange. However, for Buddhists, this way of seeing and being in the world is the cause of craving.

Buddhists would say, as you are a subject-I and everything and everyone else is an object, you will, by necessity, need to relate to the world. In relating to the people in the world, you may realize that you cannot get beyond thinking of all persons as objects even though you know that they must be subjects too—subjects who correspondingly regard you as an object-you. So, how can you regard a person both as a subject and an object? Buddhism would say that we cannot until we gain Awakening. Until then, we cannot really know a person completely, not even our spouse or child, because as hard as we try, we cannot penetrate our limitation of engaging them only as objects. There is then, a split, a gap between what they really are (both subject and object) and what I can relate to them as (only an object).

So, too, even when I think of myself, I objectify myself. That is, in stating, "I am Leslie," I am at once saying there is a subject ("I") asserting an object ("Leslie"). If I try to get to the "I" (subject-Leslie), I only end up saying something like, "I am asserting I am Leslie." Every time I try to get to the subject of another or myself, I inevitably end up objectifying and so creating an ever-regressing distance from the subject. This incompleteness in my engagement with myself is the source of suffering and dissatisfaction, or as Buddhist theologian Masao Abe puts it:

> Self-estrangement and anxiety are *not* something *accidental* to the ego-self, but are inherent to its structure. To be human ... lture, class, ... be human ... be cut off ... ut off from ... nt anxiety.
> This is the human predicament.[17]

For Buddhism, our root problem is that we do not see either ourselves or others completely or authentically. Our ordinary self-consciousness does not allow us to do so. Unlike many religions and philosophies that would agree with this analysis but not find it a problem, Buddhism believes it is the root cause of unhappiness. As the Oracle of Delphi admonished, "Know thyself." If to know oneself is the purpose of all humans, as long as we are limited by our ordinary consciousness, we will never be able to fulfill this purpose. Buddhism does suggest an answer and that is the Third Noble Truth.

The Third Noble Truth

That Buddhism provides an answer to the human problem counters the charge that Buddhism is pessimistic. If it were truly pessimistic, Buddhism would tell you that you have a problem and not give you any answer!

The answer that Buddhism provides is the Third Noble Truth, which states that craving and consequently suffering can be made to cease. This is realized when the person gains Awakening. What is Awakening?

We mentioned Awakening in passing in the opening chapter but let's expand upon those comments. In Buddhist literature, you will not find a solid definition of Awakening. This may be frustrating to us—if it is so important and the "secret" to being fully a human person, then why doesn't Buddhism tell us all about it!

Buddhism has good reasons for not spelling out the answer. First, if Buddhism simply supplied the answer then it wouldn't be our discovery. As you know, any religion that simply tells you what you should believe does not automatically make you believe. As in studying math, if the teacher provides you the answer to a problem, it does not mean you know the math. That is why your teacher always wants you to "show your work" and prove that you understand the way to solve the problem. So, too, for the Buddhist teacher who says, "Show me how you get Awakening rather than me telling you what it is like."

Still, we want to know what Awakening is and, as with the math example, it may help us show our work if we know what answers we are supposed to get. So, can we better understand the Buddhist Awakening?

It is first important to emphasize again that intellectually understanding Buddhism is not the answer. You can read every book on Buddhism ever written (which would take you a long time) but that will not help you achieve the Buddhist experience of Awakening. What is needed is an actualization rather than simply an understanding. That is, you need to experience Awakening yourself.

Remember that the problem of craving and its resulting suffering came from our ability to see the world only as objects. The answer then, for Buddhism, is to see the world completely, as subjects and objects, which Buddhism declares is the true picture of the world. Awakening to the True Self, the genuine way of being in the world, is analogous to waking from a dream that seemed real and is only dispelled as a dream when we awake and discover that it was only a dream. When Awakened, one can see the objects of the world and oneself as complete and total. The Chinese Zen Master Ch'ing-yüan Wei-hsin wrote the following quatrain that may help us better understand:

> Thirty years ago, before I began the study of Zen, I said, "Mountains are mountains, waters are waters." After I got an insight into the truth of Zen through the instruction of a good master, I said, "Mountains are not mountains, waters are not waters." But now, having attained the abode of final rest [that is, Awakening], I say, "Mountains are really mountains, waters are really waters."[18]

In the first line, we see again the subject-object distinction of ordinary consciousness. Mountains are seen as objects, that is, as discrete from waters (rivers), and I am, as the viewer of both, acting as a subject-I, looking at mountains and waters as objects.

Wei-hsin then states that after he received an insight in Zen, the "mountains were now waters, the waters mountains." Clearly in this second stage, there is a negation of the first consciousness, or as Masao Abe puts it, "we realize there is no differentiation, no objectification, . . . no duality of subject and object."[19]

Abe goes on to argue that there are two aspects to this second stage realization: first, that it marks an end to the ever-regressing objectification of self and other—the ordinary self has "died" (Zen Buddhism refers to this point as the "Great Death") and what one might call an onto-existential "block" (in Zen terminology, a "great doubt block") has been manifested as a self that has "come to a *deadlock*, and *collapse* through the *total* realization of endlessness and unattainability with its whole body and mind."[20]

The second aspect is that although the ordinary self and its objectifying nature have been extirpated and its dualistic matrix of subject-object voided, there still persists a dualistic framework between the first stage (dual) and the newly emerged second stage (nondual). In order to attain a completely nondual position, there needs to be a third movement into a consciousness that includes dual and nondual, difference and nondifference. We see this completely nondual stage in the third statement of the passage, which states, "But now, having attained the abode of final rest [that is, Awakening], I say, 'Mountains are really mountains, waters are really waters.'" Or, as we may render it, mountains are mountains *and* mountains are waters, waters are waters *and* waters are mountains, or, if one wishes to speak about persons, I am I *and* I am you [and every other thing]. This posits Awakened consciousness as a paradoxical nondualistic-dualistic consciousness, a selfless-self-consciousness that is viewed as the True Self by Zen Buddhist thought. Turning again to Masao Abe:

> Thus in the Zen Awakening attained by Wei-hsin, on the one hand, mountains are really mountains in themselves, waters are really waters in themselves—that is, everything in the world is real in itself; and yet, on the other hand, there is no hindrance between any one thing and any other thing—everything is equal, interchangeable, and interfusing.[21]

This may not clear up what Buddhism means by Awakening, and you may now see why the Buddhist tradition has avoided an explanation of the term. Explanations can become complicated when one tries to explain what can really only be experienced for oneself. Yet, perhaps an intellectual explanation may still be useful to us, as it may be useful to a Buddhist practitioner as long as he or she does not mistake having an intellectual understanding with having the actualization of Awakening. As a Zen phrase puts it, one should not mistake a finger pointing to the moon with the moon itself.

With the Great Wisdom (Mahâprajnâ) that is Awakening comes Great Compassion (Mahākaruna). What is this Great Compassion? How can it help us to understand the Buddhist Awakening?

The previous discussion on Awakening used the idea of subject and object to typify ordinary consciousness. That is to say, as we engage another person, we engage that person as an object to our consciousness. Certainly we may have different associations with that person, depending on who he or she is and how well we know him or her but nevertheless, he or she remains an object to our consciousness. The Buddhist analysis would argue that no matter how close we may get to that person in a love relationship, there still is a gulf between us. We may have moments of what one may call a nondualistic or "at-one" feeling with this other person, but these feelings do not last and fade away since they are conditioned by the separateness that typifies the subject-object matrix.

When one is Awakened, this separateness no longer typifies human relationships. It is replaced with a constant nondualistic engagement of the other that can be rendered as "fulfilled love." A love that is defined as both dual and nondual—one where the lover and the loved are both one and two, both the same yet distinct. No longer estranged from the other, the Awakened person opens his or her eyes in the morning to a unification of all things bright and beautiful. Buddhism argues that this is the desideratum for all humankind as it is the fulfillment of who we truly are as humans.

The Fourth Noble Truth: The Eightfold Path

> The Buddha replied, "Subhadda, it is not important whether they are fully enlightened. The question is whether you want to liberate yourself. If you do, practice the Noble Eightfold Path. Wherever the Noble Eightfold Path is practiced, joy, peace, and insight are there." (*Mahaparinibbana Sutta, Digha Nikaya,* 16)[22]

Now that Buddhism has revealed the answer, it needs to tell us how to get to the answer. This is called the Eightfold Path.

The Eightfold Path can be rendered in different ways, but it basically follows a pattern like this:

1) Right View

2) Right Intention

3) Right Speech

4) Right Action

5) Right Effort

6) Right Livelihood

7) Right Concentration

8) Right Mindfulness

Let's briefly examine each of these steps on the path, remembering that these are not to be approached one at a time, as if one were ascending a ladder but should rather be viewed holistically as if each were the ladder itself. As Thich Nhat Hanh put it, "Each limb contains all the other seven." [23]

Right View means that the person believes in the Buddha and his teachings. This is a very important first step because Buddhism is a religion of faith. A Buddhist needs to believe he or she too can realize an Awakening that is not a hair's difference from the experience of the Buddha. A novice practitioner takes refuge in the "Three Jewels," namely, the Buddha, the Dharma, and the Sangha.

Right Intention means that the Buddhist is practicing Buddhism for the right reasons and is not being forced to, or does not have bad motives for following the path.

Right Speech is one of the ethical (sila) steps in the Eightfold Path and it holds, as the name implies, that one should tell the truth, not gossip or engage in empty talk but rather try to speak positively and affirmatively about oneself and others.

Right Action is another ethical step. It states that the Buddhist should not engage in harmful actions such as murder, stealing, or violence of any sort. A Buddhist should seek out people of peace and seek to make peace with all living things.

Right Effort is necessary because the actualization of Awakening is a difficult task. A Buddhist must strive vigilantly, with a positive attitude and tireless resolve.

Right Livelihood means that one's job should be consistent with the Buddhist path. This step is closely connected with Right

Action. A Buddhist should not cause any sentient (conscious) being to suffer violence. This generally means a Buddhist will not hold a job as a butcher, a hunter, or a fisherperson. Nor will a Buddhist serve in the military in a role that involves harming anyone.

Right Concentration relates to Buddhist practice, specifically to the discipline of the mind. A Buddhist works to concentrate on present reality and not dwell on past events or anticipate future events. Another name for this is mindfulness. It means being fully present to each moment as one lives it. A Buddhist strives diligently to develop good concentration skills, because they are crucial to moving closer to Awakening.

Right Mindfulness occurs contemporaneously with Awakening. Until there is Awakening, one is not truly able to practice right mindfulness.

3

Scriptures

The definitive sutras [scriptures] are the wisdom sutras,
such as the Heart of Wisdom (Prajñāpāramutāahrdaya),
in which the Buddha spoke of the ultimate nature of all
phenomena: that form is emptiness and emptiness is
form, and apart from form, there is no emptiness.

—Tenzin Gyatso, His Holiness,
the Fourteenth Dalai Lama,
in *The World of Tibetan Buddhism*

EARLY BUDDHIST WRITINGS

During the Buddha's lifetime, no Buddhist texts were created. It wasn't until he passed into parinirvâṇâ that the sangha became very concerned about continuing the teachings. A short time later the leaders of the Buddhist community got together in a great meeting to share the teachings and begin to write down what they had learned.

These texts allowed Buddhism to persist even though its founder was no longer living. Furthermore, once a tradition has a written record, it becomes easier for it to move to other countries where it will be translated into other languages, thus enabling people to read the texts in their own language and offer their own interpretations of them.

Buddhism began to spread ever further as the timeline on the following page indicates. As Buddhism spread to other countries, different understandings of the Buddha's teachings emerged. With these different understandings came the birth of different types of Buddhism. Although there are many smaller subdivisions, the two primary branches of Buddhism are Theravâda Buddhism and Mahâyâna Buddhism.

THERAVÂDA AND MAHÂYÂNA BUDDHISM

The moments surrounding the death of the founder of a religion are always critical; the Buddha's parinirvâṇâ forced the sangha to determine how the movement would carry on. While still alive, the Buddha had given indications that the movement was to rely on his teachings and the discipline that had been established for the sangha.

The sangha convened in two important councils: the first in Râjagraha soon after the Buddha's death and the other a hundred years later. The task in Râjagraha was to determine the exact teachings and discipline that Buddhists were to follow and to codify them. The tradition describes this meeting as a debriefing of Ânanda and Upâli, two of the leading disciples, informing them of what the monks remembered the Buddha to have taught with respect to both doctrine and practice. These reports were

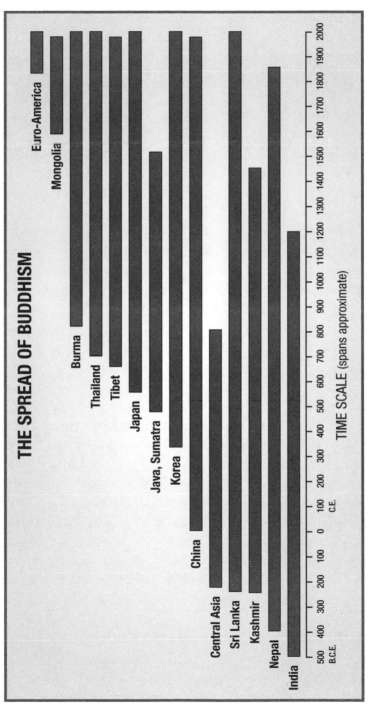

THE SPREAD OF BUDDHISM

TIME SCALE (spans approximate)

This graph shows the spread of Buddhism, beginning in India approximately 500 B.C.E. and continuing to the present day in Europe and the Americas.

passed down over time and ultimately became the Buddhist scriptures known as the *Tripitaka* ("Three Baskets"). The Tripitaka consists of three collections: the *Vinaya Pitaka*, the *Sutra Pitaka*, and the *Abhidharma Pitaka*.

The Vinaya Pitaka is basically a book of Buddhist discipline. It provides guidance on how both monastics (monks and nuns) and laypersons are to conduct themselves.

The Sutra Pitaka contains the discourses of the Buddha. In them, the Buddha discusses the main ideas of Buddhism with his followers. The Socratic question-and-answer form is seen throughout these sutras.[24]

The Abhidharma Pitaka comprises the philosophical or scholastic part of the collection. Although the Buddhist tradition ascribes this text to the recitation of Ânanda at the first council, Western historians say that it really evolved over time and only began to be composed in the fourth century B.C.E.

How does this textual history relate to the differences between Theravâda and Mahâyâna? Perhaps it isn't surprising that disagreements arose among members of the sangha in regard to the texts and their interpretation. The second council, this one in the city of Vaiśâlî, was called to deal with these disagreements, which were probably already long-standing at that time. Ultimately there was a schism of the Buddhist sangha, dividing it into two factions: the sthaviras ("seniors") and the mahâsaṅghika ("great community"). The sthaviras formed Theravâda Buddhism and the second group is connected with Mahâyâna Buddhism.

We turn now to consider the differences between the two primary branches of Buddhism. It is important to remember, however, that Theravâda and Mahâyâna have more similarities than differences. All Buddhists believe in the same basic Buddhist teachings (dharma) and in the importance of nirvana or Awakening.

THE BASIC TENETS OF MAHÂYÂNA BUDDHISM

If you are able to travel to East Asia and visit Japan, Korea, or Taiwan, you will undoubtedly see many temples that belong to Mahâyâna Buddhist sects. As you enter these temples, you will encounter statues that supposedly represent the Buddha but may look very different from one another. Statues of the Buddha not only vary widely in appearance, but they also have many different names associated with them. The sightseer may conclude that Buddhism is as polytheistic as Hinduism! Or, is it that all of these are representations of the Buddha but with different names?

To answer this question, we need to examine what transpired as Mahâyâna Buddhism began to develop. As we have mentioned, there was a schism or split in the Buddhist community that resulted in factions, one being the Mahâsaṅghika. Buddhist scholars used to maintain that this movement gave birth to the Mahâyâna movement but as Donald Mitchell notes:

> . . . more recent scholarship has noted that perhaps the Mahâyâna writings and practices actually influenced Mahâsaṅghika positions. In fact, there is evidence that Mahâyâna was not originally associated with just one sect but was a kind of "esoteric" spirituality of interest to persons in many schools.[25]

Mahâyâna literally means "great vehicle." Its viewpoint has been shaped over many centuries and many writings. For the Mahâyâna sect, the writings contained in the Tripitaka, though critically important, were not the only acceptable texts. They believed that additional texts could be canonical and important for guiding the sangha. Mahâyâna Buddhists came to see these texts as the culmination of the earlier texts and differing subgroups came to extol some texts or sutras above others. These texts contained ideas that are seminal to Mahâyâna Buddhism, and by examining a few of these ideas we can better define this type of Buddhism. The ideas we will examine are the doctrine of *Trikâya* and the *bodhisattva* ideal.

THE DOCTRINE OF TRIKÂYA

The Buddha passed into parinirvâṇâ and no longer continued his cycle of birth and rebirth. One might ask, however, why he did not return in a different body to help bring others to

Awakening. Mahâyâna Buddhist texts answered this question with the doctrine of Trikâya.

The doctrine of Trikâya posits that the Buddha actually exists in three bodies (Tri=three, kâya=body)—the body of essence (Dharmakâya), the body of bliss (Sambhogakâya), and the body of transformation (Nirmânakâya). This last body was the body that the Buddha manifested during his corporeal life on earth. However, even while in this body, there were two other levels that the Buddha simultaneously inhabited. The Sambhogakâya was the next level; on this level the Buddha dwelt in a sort of everlasting heaven. This idea expanded to

THE DHAMMAPADA

One of the most popular Buddhist texts is the Dhammapada. The title means "the path of *dharma*." The book is composed of a little more than four hundred verses on how to live a Buddhist life. It is part of the Sutra Pitaka and was presented at the First Council by Ânanda. Translations of this Theravâda text date back to the beginning of the Common Era. A few sample verses may serve to demonstrate the flavor of this text:

The quivering, wavering mind,
Hard to guard, hard to check,
The sagacious one makes straight,
Like a fletcher, an arrow shaft. (verse 33)
[A fletcher is someone who makes arrows]

By standing alert, by awareness,
By restraint and control too,
The intelligent one could make an island
That a flood could not overwhelm. (verse 25)

Engage not in unawareness,
Nor in intimacy with sensual delight.
Meditating, the one who is aware
Attains excessive ease. (verse 27)

include numerous bliss bodies that inhabit a higher plane, and that is how the various Buddhas and bodhisattvas (see following section) with their differing looks and attributes developed in Buddhism. For example, there is *Amitâbha* Buddha (Skt.)*, the Buddha venerated by Pure Land Buddhists (see page 54), and *Avalokiteśvara* (Skt.), the bodhisattva of compassion. Avalokiteśvara, also known as Kuan-yin (Ch.) and Kannon (Jp.), is often portrayed with many arms to better assist petitioners with their many tasks. Tibetan Buddhism considers the Dalai Lama to be a manifestation of this bodhisattva. It was the Sambhogakâya doctrine that allowed for the development

Let one tell the truth, let one not be angry.
Asked, let one give even when one has but little.
By these three factors,
With these three factors,
One would go into the presence of the gods. (verse 224)

Refraining from all that is detrimental,
The attainment of what is wholesome,
The purification of one's mind:
This is the instruction of the Awakened Ones. (verse 183)

When a need has arisen, friends are a blessing,
A blessing is contentment with whatever [there be],
A blessing is the wholesome deed at the end of life,
A blessing it is to relinquish all sorrow.
A blessing in the world is reverence for mother,
A blessing, too, is reverence for father . . .
A blessing is virtue into old age,
A blessing is faith established,
A blessing is the attainment of insight-wisdom,
A blessing is to refrain from doing wrongs. (verses 331–333, abridged)

(All translations are from John Ross Carter, Mahinda Palihawadana's translation, New York: Oxford University Press, 1987.)

of theistic Buddhism and its veneration of various Buddhas and bodhisattvas. In Theravâda Buddhism no attempt was made to contact the Buddha or to pray to him after his death. No one imagined him as dwelling in a heavenly realm. Theravâda Buddhism did not encourage speculation as to what happened to a Buddha after death.

The Dharmakâya was even further removed from the other bodies and was depicted as omnipresent and the substrate of the universe. The Dharmakâya, in other words, is the essence of Buddha-nature that resides in all things, animate and inanimate.

* Skt. = Sanskrit, Ch. = Chinese, Jp. = Japanese, K. = Korean

THE BODHISATTVA IDEA

A central doctrine that distinguishes Mahâyâna from Theravâda Buddhism is the idea of the bodhisattva. Bodhisattva literally means something like "being of wisdom (Awakening)." So, a bodhisattva is a being that is Awake. The bodhisattva is the ideal person in Mahâyâna Buddhism.

The Mahâyâna Buddhists forwarded the concept of the bodhisattva in opposition to the Theravâdan notion of the *arhat*. The arhat was the Theravâdan ideal person—he was someone who had burned off all his karma, like a fire burns fuel, and is then extinguished. The arhat has entered into nirvana and will never enter samsara again. The Mahâyânists thought this was a selfish way of approaching the bliss of nirvana, lacking in the Buddhist virtue of compassion. The arhat also displayed a lack of wisdom,[26] they thought, because he seemed to view entering nirvana as an individual enterprise, thereby displaying a belief in the permanence of the self. Mahâyâna depicted the arhat as a pratyeka-buddha, a person who has gained Awakening but does not communicate his or her Awakening to others. Consider this exchange between Gautama and one of his disciples Shâriputra:

What do you think, Shâriputra? Do any of the disciples and private buddhas [pratyeka-buddha] ever think: "After we have gained full enlightenment, we will bring innumerable beings . . . to complete Nirvâna?"

Certainly not, Lord!

But, said the Lord, the bodhisattva [has this resolve] . . . A firefly . . . doesn't imagine that its glow will light up all India or shine all over it, and so the disciples and private buddhas don't think that they should lead all beings to Nirvâna . . . after they have gained full enlightenment. But the disc of the sun, when it has risen, lights up all India and shines all over it. Similarly the bodhisattva . . . when he has gained full enlightenment, brings countless beings to Nirvâna.[27]

You may recall that the term Buddha means "one who is Awake." What, then, is the difference between a bodhisattva (a being who is Awake) and a Buddha? The answer that is usually given is that a Buddha is fully Awakened and a bodhisattva is Awakened but has foregone complete Awakening and, due to his or her great compassion (mahâkaruna), stays among ordinary human beings and helps guide them to Awakening. I believe it is more accurate to say that there is no distinction—Mahâyâna Buddhism used the term bodhisattva to underline the importance of the great compassionate nature of the Awakened person. Since compassion is a defining characteristic of Awakening, certainly Buddhas must have this great compassion as well.

A bodhisattva takes a vow to lead all beings to Awakening, no matter how long it takes, and no matter how often he or she needs to be reborn in samsara in order to accomplish this task. The practice of a bodhisattva focused on the Mahâyâna virtues known as the Six Perfections (pâramitâs): giving (*dâna*), morality (sila), patience (ksânti), striving (virya), meditation (*dhyâna*), and wisdom (*prajñâ*).

RELIGIO-PHILOSOPHICAL DEVELOPMENTS IN MAHÂYÂNA

Even as Mahâyâna Buddhism developed the new interpretations of the dharma that allowed theistic Buddhism to develop and flourish, it also gave rise to new philosophical treatments of Buddhism. In the remainder of this chapter, I will describe some important Buddhist schools and the most important ideas found in the scriptures of those schools. I will begin in India, followed by East Asia, then Southeast Asia, and finally Tibet. The two most important Mahâyâna philosophical systems to develop in India were those of the Mâdhyamika and the Yogâcâra schools.

Mâdhyamika

The major progenitor of the *Mâdhyamika* position was one of the greatest Buddhist thinkers in history, Nâgârjuna (ca. C.E. 150–250). Nâgârjuna posited that objects, as we perceive them in ordinary consciousness, make up a provisional reality and that, in authentic reality, all objects are emptiness (śûnyatâ).

What is emptiness? It is a doctrine that takes early Buddhist philosophy to its logical conclusion. Early Buddhism stressed that everything is impermanent. The Abhidharma philosophers interpreted the doctrine of impermanence to mean that everything was composed of real elements that continuously originated and were continuously destroyed. Nâgârjuna taught that the elements were not just impermanent, but that they lacked any real being at all. Because everything is empty of real being, Nâgârjuna's view of the world is called emptiness. Emptiness is not the same thing as nihilism (the view that existense is senseless and useless). It is closely associated with the Buddhist philosophy of the "middle way," which stated that one should steer away from extremes. Existence is one extreme, nonexistence is the other extreme. Emptiness is neither; rather, it is a teaching that demonstrates why claims to either existence or nonexistence are wrongheaded.

Another way to look at emptiness is to see it as an example of dependent co-arising (*pratîtya-samutpâda*). Everything arises dependent on causes and conditions, so nothing has "own-being" (independent existence). Objects only exist interdependently with all existence. Or, to use the language we have been using, all things are existent and nonexistent, dual and nondual simultaneously. Therefore, it is not a simple nonexistence set against existence that Nâgârjuna is elucidating here but a complete notion of emptiness that paradoxically includes both existence and nonexistence.

This kind of reasoning had implications for the traditional way in which Buddhism had opposed nirvana and samsara. These, too, were opposite extremes, just like existence and nonexistence were opposite extremes. They, too, could only exist simultaneously and interdependently. Hence the Mahâyâna teaching that nirvana is samsara, and samsara is nirvana. These were not two separate places, but two levels of truth.

Nâgârjuna's aim was to disassemble other arguments that were prevalent in his day, including the nihilistic argument. He taught that it was critical to distinguish between conventional truth and absolute truth in order to reach the experience of śûnyatâ. His theoretical writings supported developments in Buddhist logic and directly influenced *Ch'an* Buddhism (Japanese Zen Buddhism). Zen's emphasis on nonattachment to intellectual positions is a corollary of Nâgârjuna's philosophy of the two levels of truth: conventional truth and absolute truth.

Yogâcâra

Yogâcâra Buddhism taught the philosophy of "mind-only," which is often described as a form of idealism that asserts that mind or consciousness is the only reality. Yogâcâra philosophers asserted that the phenomenal world only exists in the consciousness of the perceiver. That is, if you remove the perceiver, the world does not exist.

The most significant architects of this school of thought were Maitreyanântha (ca. C.E. 270–350), the Asanga brothers (ca. 310–390), and Vasubandhu (ca. 320–400). How is it, they asked, that many different people can have the same perceptions? Furthermore, how can we explain internal visualizations like dreams that seem so real even though they are not real?

The Yogâcâra view was that there must be a common place from which these perceptions are drawn, a "storehouse" of perceptions (*âlaya-vijñâna*) that persons are able to access. Objects in this "storehouse" are similarly perceived by similar beings. As was the case with the Mâdhyamika, the Yogâcâra school of philosophy also stated that there was an authentic reality that transcended this proto-reality of perceived objects. They termed this authentic reality "suchness" (tathatâ).

In Yogâcâra philosophy, Awakening was said to occur when the duality between the "storehouse" perceptions and suchness was extirpated. Meditation and visualizations were used to achieve this nonduality.

EAST ASIAN MAHÂYÂNA BUDDHIST SCHOOLS
Buddhism in China

Although it is difficult to determine precisely when Buddhism came to China, it probably arrived in the first century of the Common Era. Its arrival presented some interesting challenges for China and for Buddhism as well.

Gautama Buddha was embraced by the Chinese court as an Indian deity and placed alongside the Taoist figure Lao-tzu. However, the relationship between the Confucian and Buddhist traditions was more challenging.

Buddhists constructed temples that were tax exempt. As these temples became more influential, native opposition and resentment grew. Buddhism had a monastic tradition, and its monks were celibate. Confucian thought, which was very family centered, disapproved of the monastic lifestyle. The Chinese took a dim view of the monks' shaven heads. Buddhist belief in rebirth was contrary to the ancestor veneration of the Chinese. The Buddhists were thoroughly imbued with the Indian virtue of ahimsa (non-harm, non-injury) and therefore did not join the military at a time when all Chinese men were subject to military duty.[28] Although the Taoists were more receptive to Buddhism, their emphasis on attaining physical immortality led them to hope that Buddhist medical knowledge would aid in that endeavor. They were disappointed that Buddhist medical knowledge did not tend in that direction. It is important to note, however, that the knowledge of herbs and healing that the

Buddhists brought with them from India was and is a significant part of their success in gaining converts.

Buddhism changed as it settled into China. Even to translate Buddhist texts into the Chinese language required knowledge of Chinese religious and cultural traditions. The translation project was monumental and continued in earnest for several centuries. By then, Buddhists were becoming Chinese as much as China was becoming Buddhist. Consequently, new forms of Buddhism developed in China.

The Chinese Buddhist schools were the heirs of the translations project. They were the new interpreters of Mahâyâna Buddhism, and they shaped both doctrine and practice in unique ways. The Chinese Buddhist schools set the stage for the advent of the Korean and Japanese schools.

Chinese Buddhist Schools
T'ien-t'ai School

The T'ien-t'ai ("Heavenly Terrace") school is sometimes referred to as the Lotus school. T'ien-t'ai Buddhists look to the Lotus Sutra as their primary text, and they consider it to be the highpoint of the Buddhist sutra tradition. Chih-i (C.E. 538–597) is extolled as the foremost interpreter of this text. The school derives its name from a mountain in Chekiang Province where Chih-i taught.[29]

T'ien-t'ai doctrine, which is Mahâyâna in flavor, stressed the importance of both meditation and philosophy. This school attempts to elucidate the "threefold truth."

The first truth is that all things are empty, including the self. The second truth states that all things have a relative or temporary reality. The third truth states that the "two realities" (the relative as discerned by ordinary consciousness and the absolute as discerned by the Awakened consciousness) are in fact one. The "threefold truth" is another way of stating the "samsara is nirvana, nirvana is samsara" argument. It also echoes our earlier description of the nondualistic-dual nature of reality.

The lokas (or levels of sentient existence—deities, animals, hungry ghosts, and so forth), which were mentioned in the karma and rebirth discussion in Chapter One, derive from T'ien-t'ai's elaboration of the relative realm of reality. More importantly, T'ien-t'ai is responsible for breaking down the Awakened-Unawakened duality by positing that all sentient beings have the Buddha nature. The claim is not simply that each person has the potential to actualize the Awakened Mind but that we all are, in fact, Awakened. As important as the distinction between the ordinary mind and the Awakened Mind is, it is a conceptual structure that posits a duality. (This is true of all conceptual structures.) Because Mahâyâna stresses the importance of nonduality, all such conceptual structures must be jettisoned once they have made their point. Beyond the duality of conceptual structures, the T'ien-t'ai Buddhist seeks *tathatâ* ("suchness"), which is the Awakened Consciousness in play. The methodology employed by T'ien-t'ai is actually a combination of meditation and devotionalism.

T'ien-t'ai is considered the first "indigenous" school of Chinese Buddhism. It subsequently was carried to Korea, where it is known as Ch'nt'ae, and to Japan, where it is called Tendai. Tendai's headquarters on Mount Hiei, just outside of Kyoto, were established by the eminent Japanese monk, Saichô.

Hua-yen School

The "Flower Garland" school of Chinese Buddhism recognizes two people as being most instrumental in its formation: Tu-Shun (557–640) and Fa-tsang (643–712). The latter played the leading role in the shaping of Hua-yen thought.

The Hua-yen school has much in common with the T'ien-t'ai school: It argues that all things are codependent, coarising, and so ultimately one. While attempting to introduce China's Empress Wu to Hua-yen philosophy, Fa-tsang used the metaphor of a golden lion. Gold, he said, has no self-nature; it is only the fact that it exists in the form of a lion that makes it something. Likewise, the form of the lion has no own-being; it is dependent upon the substance of gold to actually exist. Thus, it is only because of the interdependence between the form ("lion") and the substance (gold) that the golden lion exists as a golden lion. Neither of the elements (form or substance) can manifest without the other. Everything in the world is like the golden lion, according to Hua-yen. It has no being within itself, but only arises because of mutually arising codependent causes. The causes do not have own-being either, because neither can manifest without the other.

As we pursue this and ask, "What is the lion?" we must answer that it is gold in the shape of a lion but that materially, there is only gold. The shape of the lion does not actually exist except due to our senses of perceiving the object and our knowledge of what a lion looks like, or as Professor Donald Mitchell extols:

> [8] The lion is spoken of to demonstrate the result of ignorance, while its golden essence is spoken of in order to make clear its true nature .... [9] This lion is a created *dharma*, arising and passing away in every moment ... Yet, since the different periods of time are formed dependent on one another, they are merging harmoniously and mutually penetrating together without obstruction in each moment of time ... [10] The gold and the lion may be hidden or manifest ... but neither has any own-being. They are constantly being evolved through the transformation of the mind.[30]

If we consider the gold as emptiness and the form of the lion as the cosmos, Fa-tsang's metaphor can be extended to explain that emptiness and form arise together and this coexistence results in distinct forms. Though distinct, all forms also interpenetrate one another, influencing and conditioning each other. Hua-yen uses the image of Indra's Net to explain this mutual interpenetration. Indra's Net is a spiderweb-like net with mirrors set at each point of intersection of the threads. These mirrors reflect endlessly into and out of each other. The idea is that everything is limited in itself but simultaneously reflects all other realities.

Similarly, consider a wave on the ocean. Although the wave may seem only a small part of the ocean, a small and transient part that rises and falls, it holds within it both emptiness and form.

The Awakening comes when one sees that all phenomena are causally determined and ultimately empty. The Hua-yen school suggests meditation as the most likely means of facilitating such an Awakening.

Pure Land School

Today the Pure Land school is the most popular type of Buddhism in China, and its counterparts in Japan and Korea are the most popular schools of Buddhism in those countries. It is a devotional form of Buddhism, emphasizing faith and devotion as vehicles to liberation rather than meditation or philosophy.

The Chinese name for this school is Ching-t'u. A particular Buddha named Amitâbha stands at the center of Ching-t'u's belief system. The Pure Land Scripture tells the story of Amitâbha, once a bodhisattva named Dharmâkara. En route to his Awakening, Dharmâkara took forty-eight vows. The eighteenth vow reads:

> If, O Blessed One, when I have attained enlightenment, whatever beings in other worlds, having conceived a desire for right, perfect enlightenment, and having heard my name, with favorable intent think upon me, if when the time and moment of death are upon them, I, surrounded by and at the head of my community of mendicants, do not stand before them to keep them from frustration, may I not, on that account, attain to unexcelled, right, perfect enlightenment.[31]

As Dharmâkara did in fact become a Buddha, the recitation of his name became the primary practice of Buddhists in this school. Anyone seeking to join Amitâbha in the Pure Land (which is also called the Western Paradise) is to recite "A-mi-t'o-fo" (in Chinese).

Since Buddhism began as a movement emphasizing monasticism, meditation, and philosophy, why is it that the most popular form of Buddhism today emphasizes none of those things but only faith and devotion? Buddhists have their theories as to why this has happened. Believers in Mahâyâna Buddhism frequently hold that the dharma is strongest when a Buddha is present on Earth, but after the Buddha leaves there is a period of degeneration in the dharma. During Siddhartha Gautama's lifetime, the dharma was at its pinnacle and many people were able to reach nirvana. Now, however, we are in the final degenerative phase of the dharma, referred to in Japanese as the *mappô*. Given these circumstances, the only real chance that believers have to attain nirvana is to generate faith in Amitâbha's beneficence and call on his name.

Ch'an: The Meditation School

In the West, one of the best-known Buddhist schools is that of Zen Buddhism; however, Zen traces its heritage back to the Chinese meditation school known as Ch'an. Ch'an means "meditation," as does dhyana and Zen. So, not surprisingly, the primary practice of Ch'an Buddhist believers is meditation.

Meditation had been a spiritual practice in Asia for many centuries; dating back at least as far as the earliest beginnings of Hinduism. A stone stamp with the unmistakable image of a person in the lotus meditation position (both legs folded over one's thighs in a seated position) has been traced to the Indus Civilization that predates the Aryan incursion into India (ca. 1500 B.C.E.). Yoga as it subsequently developed in India maintained the use of seated meditation as part of a spiritual practice.

Among the Buddhist schools, it was Ch'an Buddhism that elevated meditation to the position of being its central practice. Meditation was given a status even higher than that of the scriptures. Indeed, Ch'an is often described as:

> A special transmission outside the scriptures;
> With no dependence upon words and letters;
> A direct pointing into the mind;
> Seeing there one's own nature and attaining Buddhahood.[32]

Ch'an Buddhism places utmost importance on the master-student relationship. The master stands as the living expression of Awakening and he or she drives and verifies the student's advancement toward the realization of a mind that is and yet is not different from the master's mind. In Ch'an Buddhism, the journey toward Awakening is a mind-to-mind transmission that is not scripturally derived or sanctioned.

Different methodologies are employed by Ch'an teachers to move the student from an unawakened state to Awakening. One of the best known is the kung-an (Jp.: *koan*). The kung-an (literally, "public record or case") has been defined many ways but perhaps most directly by Richard DeMartino, who said, "A koan is a Zen presentation in the form of a Zen challenge." [33]

Over time, encounters between Ch'an masters and their students began to be recorded. By the eleventh century, written collections of these encounters were being used and commented on by masters and students.[34] It was through the teachings of such masters as Dahui (1089–1163), Daitô (1282–1336), and Hakuin (1686–1769), that koans came to be seen as the major element in instruction in Ch'an Buddhism in China and Zen Buddhism in Japan.

Ch'an traces the history of the koan and its contextual mondo (dialogue between a master and a student) all the way back to Gautama Buddha and the "exchange" he had with one of his foremost students, Kashyapa, on Vulture Peak. It seems that an audience had gathered and was waiting for the Buddha to speak. The Buddha did not say a word but merely held up a flower. In response, Kashyapa smiled, and the Buddha knew he had understood. The Buddha's Awakening had been passed on to Kashyapa.[35]

This is regarded as the first transmission of the Ch'an lineage. The Ch'an lineage became a patriarchal tradition in China and subsequently an organizational lineage. Ch'an masters trace their linage, their dharma transmission, back to this patriarchal lineage. This structure acts to legitimize the master's Awakening experience and provides an organizing framework for Ch'an.

As Ch'an continued to develop in China, a Southern school and a Northern school emerged, giving rise to two different types of Ch'an. The Southern school eventually gave rise to a school that prized silent, seated meditation (the Ts'ao-tung school). In Japan, this school was popularized by Dôgen (1200–1253), where it became known as Sôtô Zen Buddhism.

The Northern School gave rise to the Lin-chi school, founded by Lin-chi (d. 867). This school was renowned for its use of koans. Lin-chi influenced the Korean school called Son. Eisai (1141–1215) brought the version known as Rinzai Buddhism to Japan.

Buddhism in Korea

Buddhism officially entered the Korean Peninsula in the fourth century (although there is a good possibility that Buddhism was unofficially present prior to that time). In the fourth century, Korea consisted of three kingdoms: Koguryô, Paekche, and Silla. Korea and China had fashioned a pact, and Shun-tao, a Chinese Buddhist monk, took advantage of the new relationship between the two countries and traveled to Koguryô.

Buddhism arrived in Paekche in C.E. 384 and was adopted as the state religion of Silla in 527. In the seventh century, the kingdom of Silla conquered both Koguryô and Paekche, inaugurating a unification that would last until 918. This political stability assisted in the development of Korean Buddhism; devotional Buddhism in particular increased in popularity.

The development of Korean Buddhism took an interesting path. Five Buddhist schools were established: three transplanted Chinese schools and two indigenous Korean schools. Ch'ont'ae (T'ien-t'ai), Son (Ch'an), and tantric practices were present as well. Despite the presence of all these various forms of Buddhism, Korea strove for unification of Buddhism within its borders. In the eleventh century, Uich'on, a notable scholar, worked toward such a unification. Perhaps the preeminent Buddhist figure in Korean history, Chinul (1158–1210), should also be mentioned for his contributions to unification.

Chinul was a religious reformer. He entered a Son Buddhist monastery as a novice when he was young. However, Chinul basically educated himself in the sutras and the practice of meditation.

Chinul longed to create a sangha where a purer form of Buddhism could be practiced. Over his lifetime, he worked toward that goal. In a series of Awakening experiences, Chinul's vision of this sangha gained increased clarity. He shaped an approach to Buddhism that combined meditation and sutras, utilized the *hwadu* (Jp.: koan) methodology, and supported the growth of Pure Land Buddhism in Korea. His vision greatly affected the development of Buddhism in Korea; his influence continues to this day.

Buddhism in Japan

Buddhism came to the Japanese Islands approximately in the middle of the sixth century via Korea. Japan presented Buddhism with a new and a very different situation than what it had seen in India or in China. Japan had an indigenous religious tradition, Shinto, but it lacked a textual tradition and many other attributes of the Indian and Chinese civilizations. In fact, Buddhism brought tremendous change to Japan, not only in religion, but by introducing myriads of forms of culture and art, primarily of Chinese origin. The entirety of the Japanese aesthetic, from architecture to the language, was affected dramatically.

As Buddhism spread from country to country, whether or not it was adopted or not often depended largely on whether it was able to attract the sponsorship of an influential leader. Japan was no exception: Prince Shôtoku (574–622) was the figure who stood at the forefront of Buddhist history in Japan. In his famed "Seventeen Article Constitution," he implored all Japanese to revere the "Three Treasures"[36] of Buddhism.

Prince Shôtoku authored commentary on Buddhist sutras and was responsible for building the first significant Buddhist temples in Japan. One of these is Horyûji (607) in Nara, where one can still see incredible examples of Buddhist art, including the Kudara Kannon. The Kudara Kannon has been designated a national treasure. It is a carving of the bodhisattva of mercy (Kannon). We do not know who created it, or when it was carved, but it is called the Kudara Kannon because a legend says that it came from the ancient Korean kingdom of Kudara (Paekche). The nearby Chûgû-ji monastery (a women's monastery) houses a Miroku (Skt.: *Maitreya*) that still attracts many Buddhist pilgrims. Maitreya is the future Buddha, who many believe will arrive on earth after Gautama Buddha's teachings have disappeared. Maitreya is derived from the Sanskrit *maitri*, meaning "universal love."

Japanese Buddhist Schools

The expansion of Buddhism into Japan occurred during several active periods. The early establishment of Buddhist schools occurred during the Nara period (710–784), so-called because Nara was the capital at the time. Six schools (Kusha, Jôjitsu, Ritsu, Sanron, Hossô, and Kegon) established their residency there. All six were based on Chinese schools. The great temple complex, Todaiji, was also built at this time (we will examine Todaiji more closely when we examine Buddhist temples in Chapter Five). During the Nara period, Japan also made its first connections with other Buddhist schools that would prove to be more enduring and influential—the Tendai and Zen schools. It was in the subsequent Heian period (794–1185), when the capital of Japan was moved from Nara to nearby Kyoto, that there was a rich development of the Tendai and Shingon schools. During the third period of note, the Kamakura period (1185–1333), the Pure Land, Zen, and Nichiren schools flourished. It might be argued that post-World War II Japan merits consideration as a fourth period, because it has seen the growth of newer expressions of Buddhism such as the Sôka Gakkai movement.

We lack the space to consider all the Japanese Buddhist schools, but, in order to get the flavor of Japanese Buddhism, let's look briefly at the Shingon, Pure Land, Zen, and Nichiren schools.

Shingon School

Atop Mount Kôya in Japan, one can walk through the darkened forest of immense cypress trees—with thousands of tombs on either side of the stone path—toward the tomb of Kûkai (774–835). His tomb, called the Gobyô, lies at the end of the path behind the Tôrô-dô Hall, a temple lit with hundreds of lamps. It is said that Kûkai retreated to this cave and still resides there in meditation rather than death. Pilgrims and tourists travel from all over Japan to visit this sacred spot and even Japanese people who do not follow Shingon Buddhism know very well the name of Kûkai. Who was this man and what is Shingon?

Kûkai, who was posthumously given the honorary title Kobô Daishi ("propagator of the dharma"), developed the Shingon school. His own studies led him to the conclusion that Japanese Buddhism of his day was not satisfactory and that a modification was necessary. He traveled to China where he was trained in tantric[37] practice and was ordained to teach. He returned to Japan (806) and ultimately was allowed by the emperor to build a temple on Mount Kôya.

Shingon (literally, "True Word") is an esoteric tradition. It claims that its teachings come from the Dharmakâya Buddha, whereas other forms of Buddhism receive their teachings from Siddhartha Gautama, the Nirmânakâya Buddha (see "The Doctrine of Trikâya" on pages 43–46). In Shingon Buddhism, the Dharmakâya Buddha is called Vairocana. Recall that the Dharmakâya is the essence of Buddha nature that resides in all things.

This leads to the central teaching of Shingon, which is that one becomes a Buddha with one's current physical body. One does not become a Buddha after one has died, nor does one become a Buddha through one's mind alone, but rather this present living, physical body is able to attain Buddhahood. We see here the influence of Tantrism, which underscores the utility of the passions in attaining nirvana. When one becomes a Buddha in this very body, one's body becomes the body of the Buddha, one's speech becomes the speech of the Buddha, and one's mind becomes the mind of the Buddha. In Shingon

Buddhism, the Mahâyâna teaching of nonduality is used to argue that human beings are not distinct from the Buddha. We all have the Buddha nature.

Tantric practices are used to realize one's own Buddha-nature. These include the use of *mandalas, mantras,* and *mudras.* A mandala is a picture or any symbolic representation of the universe (or a part of the universe). It is used in meditation. Shingon reveres two mandalas that were brought to Japan from China by Kûkai. Both contain all of the buddhas meditated on in Shingon Buddhism, with Vairocana Buddha at the center. Each mandala is a schematic portrait of the world as seen with the eyes of perfect wisdom. A mantra is a verbal formula. Magical properties are often ascribed to mantras. Mudras are hand positions used in meditation and in iconography. The point is to use these instruments to penetrate the Dharmakâya, the enveloping Awakened nature of the universe, so that the person meditating can dissipate the erroneous belief that his or her Buddha nature is different from the reality of Dharmakâya (Vairocana Buddha). As with all tantric practice, the believer requires the guidance of a tantric master who can introduce rituals at an appropriate level as the believer progresses on the path.

The Shingon sect is not one of the larger Buddhist sects, but the Japanese people know the name of Kûkai due to his skill at calligraphy (Jp.: *Shôdo*), poetry, and his overall learnedness. Many of them live near one of the countless wells or springs ascribed to Kûkai's mystical power to produce water by striking the ground with his staff in thanksgiving for a drink of water given when he was thirsty. In Japan, Kûkai has been the subject of countless biographies and folklore.

Pure Land School

As we have seen, Pure Land Buddhism originated in China. Its primary orientation, devotion to Amitâbha Buddha (Amida Buddha in Japanese), persisted when it spread to Japan. There were several notable contributors to the development of the Pure Land school (Jp.: *Jôdo*) in Japan, including such luminaries as Kûya (903–972), Ryûnin (1072–1132), and Geshin (942–1017). But inarguably the two dominant personalities of Pure Land Buddhism in Japan were Hônen (1133–1212) and his disciple, Shinran (1173–1263).

Hônen argued that Pure Land was superior to all other forms of Buddhism. In Japanese, the difference between Pure Land and other Buddhist sects can be rendered as the difference between depending on the power of the self (*jiriki*) as opposed to the power of the other (*tariki*). Pure Land was the latter, for a Pure Land believer relied entirely upon Amida for his or her salvation. Hônen did advocate the use of the *nembutsu*, which is the repetition of Amida's name (*Namu Amida Butsu*—Praise Amida Buddha). As Hônen wrote in a final note two days before his death:

> The method of final salvation that I have propounded is neither a sort of meditation, such as has been practiced by many scholars in China or Japan, nor is it a repetition of the Buddha's name by those who have studied and understood the deep meaning of it. It is nothing but the mere repetition of the "*Namu Amida Butsu*," without a doubt of His mercy, whereby one may be born into the Land of Perfect Bliss.[38]

Shinran was a disciple of Hônen. Both had suffered persecution due to their teachings, including banishment. Shinran's mission was to carry out what his master had started, but he was willing to reach even further than Hônen in order to spread their teachings to the ordinary person.

Shinran taught that the efficacy of the Nembutsu resides not in the numerous repetitions of the words but in the earnestness of the speaker. He inveighed against the presumed usefulness of honoring other Buddhas and bodhisattvas and the monastic path. He initiated the practice of allowing monastics to marry; a practice that persists in Japan today.

Zen School

As mentioned previously, Zen is the Japanese term for meditation. This Japanese school derives from Indian and Chinese sects. In the West, Zen is much better known than Ch'an, because it was Japanese teachers who brought this form of Buddhism to the West. As was the case with Pure Land, there are once again two dominating personalities in the development of Japanese Zen. They are Eisai (1141–1215) and Dôgen (1200–1253).

Eisai began his study of Buddhism at Mount Hiei among the Tendai practitioners. He determined that a trip to China was vital to his development as a monk, and in fact he traveled there twice. Since the Ch'an school was the only school of note at the time in China, he studied in a Ch'an temple. He returned in 1191 as an ordained Ch'an teacher in the Lin-chi school (Jp.: *Rinzai*).

Eisai did much to popularize Zen in Japan. He accomplished this by aligning himself with the power of the shogun[39] and by upsetting the political tactics of the competing twelfth- and thirteenth-century Buddhist schools. The Rinzai school employed the koan method along with strict discipline to support the monks' quest for Awakening.

Dôgen's early life was a mixture of good fortune and tragedy. He enjoyed a privileged birth into an aristocratic family and received a corresponding education that prepared him well for a life of study. Unfortunately, he suffered the loss of both of his parents—his father at the age of two, his mother at the age of seven—and this likely played a large part in his decision to seek a religious life.

Like Eisai, he became a monk and studied at Mount Hiei. He found it wanting and unable to answer his questions, so he left the Tendai sect. Dôgen sought out Eisai at Kennin-ji Temple just down the mountain from Hiei in Kyoto. He was struck by Eisai's teachings but Eisai died the following year. So Dôgen studied with Myôzen, one of Eisai's students who had received the transmission of the dharma from his master. It was with Myôzen that Dôgen, at age twenty-three, journeyed to China to seek further training. He even studied at the temple (T'ien-t'ung) where Eisai had labored in China but still remained dissatisfied. Fortunately, a new master came to this temple, Ju-ching (1163–1228), and it was this relationship that proved the catalyst for Dôgen's Awakening.

Dôgen subsequently returned to Japan in 1227 and established the Sôto Zen school there. He carried on a teaching career until he passed into parinirvâṇâ. He authored several notable writings, his most famous work being the *Shôbôgenzô Zuimonki*. He also established the major training temple for the sect at Eihei-ji, a temple compound in Fukui-ken.

Dôgen's methodology can be distinguished from that of the Rinzai school by its pronounced use of shinkan-taza, which simply means to sit. The koan system was not employed systematically within the Sôto school. As Dôgen wrote, "In the pursuit of the Way [Buddhism] the prime essential is sitting (*zazen*) . . ."[40]

Nichiren School

Unlike the other Japanese Buddhist schools we have considered, Nichiren Buddhism has no predecessors in China or India. The school is named after its founder, Nichiren (1222–1282), who, like the founders of the other Japanese schools we have considered, studied at Mount Hiei. Nichiren did not view himself as the progenitor of a new form of Buddhism but as someone who was attempting to restore a Japanese Buddhism that had strayed.

Nichiren asserted that the key text for Buddhist revival was the Lotus Sutra. Correspondingly, the operative mantra should be, Namu Myôhô Renge Kyô, which means, "Praise the mysterious law of the Lotus Sutra." This claim for the Lotus Sutra, which reflected the Tendai position, was not well received by the clerical and martial powers of the time. Nichiren was persecuted and ultimately banished. The fact that he was confrontational about his beliefs did not help his situation.

Nichiren espoused three other important ideas: (1) that Japan occupied a central place in redemption for the world, (2) that we were indeed in mappô, a period of degeneration of the dharma that could only be combated by drastic, immediate action, and (3) that he had a mission to be a prophet to the masses. Nichiren Buddhism persists in Japan today, most obviously in the form of new religious movements like Sôka Gakkai ("Value-creating Society") and Risshô Kôsei-kai ("Society for the Perfection of the Nation and of the Community of Believers in Accordance with Buddhist Principles").

THERAVÂDA BUDDHISM IN SOUTHEAST ASIA

Theravâda Buddhism is found today in such countries as Myanmar, Cambodia, Sri Lanka, Laos, and Thailand. According to the *Tripitika*, Gautama Buddha said that Buddhism was to spread throughout the world. This validated the sending of Buddhist missionaries to regions outside of Northeast India. The Indian King Aśoka sent missionaries to the west and, in approximately C.E. 247, he sent some to Sri Lanka. This began the eastward migration of Theravâda Buddhism and it was also the advent of Buddhism as a world religion.

Theravâda Buddhism understands itself to be the original, unchanged form of Buddhism. Theravâdans assert that their teachings and practice are exactly as Gautama Buddha intended. This form of Buddhism looks to the Tripitaka alone for its guidance and eschews the addition of other canonical texts.

As we discussed in the Eightfold Path, the elements of morality, concentration, and wisdom are the larger categories. The Theravâdan believer works within the three important areas of morality, concentration, and wisdom to bring about his or her Awakening. Morality includes right action, right speech, and right livelihood, all of which are part of the Noble Eightfold Path. There are precepts forbidding harming life, lying, stealing, sexual immorality, and consuming forbidden substances like alcohol. The application of these precepts differs depending upon whether one is a monk or a layperson. For example, monks must practice celibacy whereas laypersons must limit their sexual relations to their marital partner. For the Theravâdan (and for a Mahâyâna Buddhist as well), the culmination of living morally occurs when one instinctively acts ethically. At that point, one no longer requires a rigid code of conduct with implicit or explicit threats of punishment for transgressions, but rather one naturally does what is right.

Likewise, the closer one draws toward Awakening, the more natural the practice of concentration and wisdom becomes. However, the development of these virtues requires long and strenuous practice. For that reason, Theravâda Buddhists maintain that the monastic life, which allots a large proportion of time to meditation and study of the scriptures, is most conducive to the development of concentration and wisdom. Only monks are expected to attain Awakening in their current lifetime, but laypersons are encouraged to build good karma so that they may perhaps become monks in their next lifetime.

VAJRAYÂNA BUDDHISM

Over the past several decades, Westerners have shown an increasing interest in Vajrayâna Buddhism. The plight of the Tibetan refugees, led by their popular spokesman, the Dalai Lama, has certainly played a large role in this expanded interest. The Dalai Lama and also many other lamas (teachers) from Tibet have visited one or more of the Western nations and established a following. Some have promulgated Vajrayâna teachings and practices by writing books in English. Consequently, Westerners now have more access to information about Vajrayâna Buddhism than in any previous period in history. Increased access has certainly helped to promote increased interest in Vajrayâna, but another reason for Western curiosity about this form of Buddhism is the fact that it has secret rituals, some of which involve activities normally forbidden by the Buddhist moral code (more about this in a while).

Vajrayâna is also sometimes called Tibetan Buddhism because that is the country with which it is most closely associated. Some religious studies scholars classify it as a type of Mahâyâna Buddhism, because it accepts additional scriptures beyond the Tripitaka, embraces the ideas of the trikâya and the bodhisattva and is in other ways similar to Mahâyâna. However, other scholars consider it to be in a category all its own because of its unique geographic setting (Tibet rather than East Asia), and because of its many distinct beliefs and practices, as will be explained below.

Schools of Vajrayâna Buddhism

Buddhism arrived relatively late in Tibet as compared with the rest of Asia. With the coming to power of Songtsen Gampo (ca. 617–649), Buddhism had an opportunity to gain a foothold. The first Buddhist temple in Tibet was constructed during his reign. In the same time period, linguistic and scholarly efforts that would allow Buddhist texts and ideas to be transmitted to the Tibetan people were promoted.

Under Songtsen Gampo, Tibet expanded in all four directions and became an important Asian power. This king was Tibet's first lawgiver, handing down ten moral rules and sixteen rules of public conduct. He sent seventeen Tibetans to India to learn Sanskrit and Buddhism. The most famous of these, Thonmi Sambhota, created the Tibetan alphabet and grammar on the basis of two Indian scripts and translated several important Buddhist texts from Sanskrit into Tibetan.

Songtsen Gampo was married to two foreign princesses, one from Nepal and the other from China, both of whom brought with them a treasured statue of Gautama Buddha. The Government of Tibet in Exile is very proud that both of these statues have been preserved, although one had to be repaired. Considering that Tibet had more than six thousand monasteries prior to the Cultural Revolution (1966–1976)—during which China attempted to suppress Tibetan nationalism—and of those only thirteen survived the revolution, it is indeed amazing that both statues dating from Songtsen Gampo's seventh-century court survived.

Trisong Detsen (ca. 742–798), who came to power in 755, was also a patron of Buddhism. He invited famous Indian Buddhist teachers to Tibet, and with their help he had Tibet's first Buddhist monastery built at Samye (consecrated 775). He presided over debates between Indian and Chinese Buddhist scholars and decided who had won. During his reign, many more Buddhist texts were translated from Sanskrit into Tibetan and the first Tibetan Buddhist monks were initiated.

Lang Dharma (r. 841–846) provides an example of a Tibetan king who opposed Buddhism and worked to suppress it. His reign culminated in a domestic upheaval that fragmented Tibet. Buddhism emerged diminished but still vital.

Over a century later, Buddhism's second opportunity for growth in Tibet was led by the esteemed Indian scholar, Atiśa (982–1054). Atiśa combined elements of Theravâda, Mahâyâna, and Tantrism. His approach proved to be very popular and dramatically shaped the distinctive character of Tibetan Buddhism. Atiśa's formulation of Buddhism led to the initial Tibetan school of Buddhism, Kadam. Two other schools soon followed, the Sakya and Kagyu. The latter was founded by another notable educator, Marpa (1012–1096), who was the teacher of the even more famous Milarepa (1040–1123).

A fourth school, Nyingma, was an orthodox response to the formation of these "new" schools. It based its teachings and practice on ancient texts. (Nyingma means "Ancient School.")

With the development of internal schools and the compilation of the Tibetan canon, Buddhism was firmly established in Tibet. Perhaps you are wondering to which of these four schools the Dalai Lama belongs. The answer is that he belongs to none of them. There is yet one more school to be considered—the Dalai Lama's school.

The Geluk School

Tsong Khapa (1357–1419) was a follower of the Kadam school but as a result of his own Awakening experience, he worked to create a new school that would articulate a syncretistic vision for Buddhism. (Recall that Atiśa had done something similar.) Initially called "New Kadam," this school was eventually renamed the Geluk school.

Tsong Khapa's successor was Gendün Drubpa (1391–1474). Drubpa is believed to have transmigrated as Gendün Gyatso (1475–1542). Gyatso subsequently was reborn as Sönam Gyatso, who, in an encounter with the Mongol warlord Altan Khan, received the Mongolian name "Dalai," which means "ocean" and implies deep wisdom. As Sönam Gyatso was viewed as the third rebirth, he is referred to as the third Dalai Lama. The current Dalai Lama, Tenzin Gyatso, is the fourteenth Dalai Lama. That is to say, the current Dalai Lama is considered the transmigration of the first Dalai Lama who has continued through many lives. The Dalai Lama is also believed to be an emanation of Avalokiteśvara, the bodhisattva of compassion. Following the bodhisattva ideal, the Dalai Lama continues to return to the human realm in order to assist all sentient beings to reach Awakening.

Vajrayâna Methodology

Vajrayâna Buddhism is distinguished by its emphasis on Tantrism. You may have heard this term before. Forty or fifty years ago, there was a great flurry of interest in Tantrism as people associated it with esoteric sexual practices. One can still find books extolling the virtues of tantric sexual practice. The connection between Tantrism and sexual practices is not entirely wrong, but it is important not to form a one-sided image of Tantrism. Rather than being one-dimensional, Tantrism is a system of great complexity and depth.

The term *tantra* (Tibetan: *rgyud*) refers to systems of practice and meditation derived from esoteric texts emphasizing cognitive transformation through visualization, symbols, and rituals.[41] The different schools of Tibetan Buddhism mentioned previously have their own versions of tantric elements.

It is important to remember that tantric practices are esoteric (meaning "private," "secret," or "confidential"). They are private practices that are given to a student by a master only when the student is thoroughly prepared. They are therefore not to be used by everyone or without the supervision of a qualified teacher. Given this, one can immediately see that the popularization of Tantrism in the West poses a problem for genuine Tantrism. Although credible masters have written books describing tantric practices for the layperson, some of the tantric practices are in fact dangerous to practice apart from the guidance of a gifted teacher. Perhaps the best one can say is that it is a changing situation, and one wonders what the implications are for Tantrism's future. As Professor John Powers wisely remarked:

> Although tantra is generally considered in Tibet to be the culmination of Buddhist teachings, it is not suitable for everyone. Tantric practice is a powerful and effective means of bringing about spiritual transformation, but for this very reason it is also thought to be dangerous. Thus Tibetan teachers contend that it is only suitable for certain exceptional individuals, while others should follow the slower but less dangerous path of the Mahâyâna sutra system or Hinayâna.[42]

The general organizing principle of Tantrism is inspired by the experience of Awakening. As all things are ultimately the same, and samsara is not different from nirvana, all efforts to separate practice from attainment, sacred from secular, and delusion from Awakening are necessarily wrongheaded. Better to incorporate the perceived antithetical elements into one's practice than to perpetuate their perceived independent reality. Furthermore, every action, whether it be as noble as a heroic deed or as mundane as going to the bathroom, can be incorporated into tantric practice. How, then, does one practice Tantrism?

It is very important to understand that genuine tantric practice depends upon the involvement of a teacher who has been trained in a recognized spiritual lineage. The teacher guides the student through stages in his or her practice, beginning with initiation. The primary purpose of initiation is to establish a strong bond between the teacher and the student. An initiation ritual should only be undertaken by a serious-minded student who is able to keep the details of the initiation ritual secret. Other "preliminary practices" include the taking of refuges ("I take refuge in the Buddha, I take refuge in the dharma, I take refuge in the sangha"), prostration, and meditation:

Tantric initiation is often a complex ritual involving detailed visualizations, prayers and supplications, offerings, special ritual implements and substances. The purpose is to establish the initiate in the proper frame of mind, forge a karmic bond with the lama [teacher] and meditational deity, purify defilements, grant permission to practice a particular tantra, and to give instruction concerning how this should be done.[43]

In the quote above, a meditational deity was mentioned. A meditational deity is a central element in deity yoga, an important tantric practice. Deity yoga involves a practitioner visualizing him or herself as an Awakened deity, such as Avalokiteśvara (Tibetan: *Chenrenzig*). Buddhists ascribe great power to the mind—one becomes what one thinks about or is influenced by. As the student meditates on Avalokiteśvara and learns to habitually think in this way, the consciousness of the visualizer (the person meditating) and the visualized (Avalokiteśvara) become one.

There are four types of tantric practice: action, performance, yoga, and highest yoga. These types can be said to constitute a progression toward nonduality. In action Tantrism, one visualizes oneself as the servant of the deity; in performance, as the friend or companion of the deity; and yoga and highest yoga involve actual nondualistic consciousness with the deity.

The use of sexuality in Tantrism deserves a further word. A few rituals prescribe the use of a partner, a "seal." The practitioner and partner are visualized "as specific deities, and one's sexual union is used as a way of generating very subtle minds."[44] This practice is reserved for very advanced practitioners who have attained a higher level in the yoga tantras. In certain ritual practices, the "seals" used are imaginary and in others they are actual persons.

SYMBOLS OF TANTRISM

In our previous discussion on Shingon, I mentioned the tantric elements of mandalas, mantra, and mudra. Some of these mandalas, or symbols of Tantrism, are becoming more familiar in the West. In the Minneapolis Museum of Art, one can find a sand mandala preserved in a case. Increasingly, one sees mandalas represented on posters or in books.

A mandala is "a diagram used in tantric meditation as an aid to visualization, which represents the residence and perfected attributes of a Buddha."[45] The tantric practitioner uses the mandala to strengthen the awareness of his or her own spiritual identity by concentrating on this articulated celestial realm. The purpose of this practice is to overcome the dualistic distinction between the visualized and the visualizer.

The mantra serves a similar purpose. Perhaps you have heard of the Hindu syllable "Om"—this is a mantra that has gained some degree of recognition in the West. Whereas the mandala is a visual aid, the mantra is a verbal aid. It is a spoken or chanted formula that invokes a deity. Once again, the idea is to overcome the misperceived distinction between the deity and oneself.

The mudra is a body movement or gesture. For example, in many Buddhist statues one will see the deity with a raised palm. This gesture, termed abhaya mudra, is meant to convey peace and it carries the meaning "Fear not!" There are many other gestures, and seated and standing positions, that convey a certain meaning. In tantric practice, the person will use these movements ritually. In fact, the practitioner often combines the mudra, mantra, and mandala in one ritual thereby unifying the body, speech, and mind.

There are other notable symbols of tantric practice that are used in Tibet as well as in esoteric Chinese and Japanese sects. One of these is the symbol that gives Vajrayâna Buddhism its name: a thunderbolt-scepter that Tibetans call a vajra. The vajra "symbolize (as absolute weapons) the victorious power of knowledge over ignorance, of the spirit over the passions . . . They are considered to annihilate spiritual poisons and to be an effective weapon against evil thoughts and desires."[46] One can find the vajra represented with different numbers of points (there is a three-pointed vajra and also a five-pointed vajra).

Worldview

He who takes refuge with Buddha,
the Law, and the Church;
he who, with clear understanding,
sees the four holy truths:
pain, the origin of pain,
the destruction of pain,
and the eight-fold holy way that
leads to the quieting of pain;
—that is the safe refuge,
that is the best refuge;
having gone to that refuge,
a man is delivered from all pain.

—The Buddha, "The Buddha—Awakened"

Buddhism developed in South Asia, so it is not surprising that Buddhism adopted some South Asian religious ideas. Karma, rebirth, ahimsa—all of these ideas existed prior to the time of Siddhartha Gautama. Hinduism and Jainism were the two most significant pre-Buddhist religions to use these ideas.

Buddhism also developed some notions that were uniquely its own—the concepts of anatman (no-self), of śûnyatâ (emptiness), of Awakening, and of the Buddha may serve as examples of these. As is the case in most religions, some of Buddhism's key concepts are unique and some are shared. The distinctively Buddhist worldview contains some of both types of concepts. In this chapter, we examine some of the distinguishing features of Buddhism that collectively shape its view of the world.

THE THREE CHARACTERISTICS OF EXISTENCE

Buddhism speaks of the three characteristics or marks of existence. These are: 1) impermanence (anicca), 2) suffering (dukkha), and 3) no-self (anatman). We have mentioned these terms before, but let us take a moment to underscore the significance of each to the Buddhist worldview.

Life Is Suffering

Recall from our discussion of the Four Noble Truths that dukkha means suffering or unsatisfactoriness. The idea that there is something "wrong" with life is certainly not unique to Buddhism. All religions are transformative, that is, they try to move us from an imperfect present condition to a better future condition. If something were not wrong—if we were not sinners, or ignorant, or mortal, or suffering, etc.—there would be no reason to get started on a religious path. But, even though Buddhism's emphasis on the trouble with life is not unique, it is a very important and pervasive part of the Buddhist worldview.

Buddhism shares Hinduism's belief that every thought or action arises because of desire. "Desire makes the world go 'round" could be the theme song of both of these religions. But whereas Hinduism sees this world as a "middle place," with some pleasure and some pain, Buddhism underscores the connection between desire and suffering. The very fact that we *desire*, rather than feel contentment or fulfillment, indicates that something is not right. This insight, which grounds the Buddhist worldview, provides a powerful incentive to get started on the Buddhist path so that things might improve.

Impermanence, Emptiness
Early Buddhism underscored the impermanence of all elements of existence, and Mahâyâna stressed the "emptiness" or lack of "own-being" of all phenomena. Both are ways of pointing to Buddhism's conviction that there is no changeless, permanently enduring reality. Everything comes into being, reaches a point of fullest development, and then fades out of existence. Or, as this truth is otherwise stated, everything arises depending on causes and conditions and does not persist in the absence of those causes and conditions.

Unlike many other religions, Buddhism does not posit any unchanging reality. It has no unchanging God or eternal soul. Buddhism offers no base on which we might affix a permanent identity for ourselves or for anything else. For this reason, there is no reason to get "attached" to anything. Buddhists attempt to act mindfully in the moment; they do not attempt to secure a permanent future state. Life, for a Buddhist, can only be meaningfully lived in the here and now. If we try to live in the past or for the future, we are not paying attention to the only reality we can really have, and that is the reality that is right here and right now.

Anatman (No-Self)
The Buddhist notion of no-self is not only a central doctrine of Buddhism but also one that is frequently misunderstood. As we study the idea of no-self, reflect back on our discussion of Awakening and the subject-object dilemma.

When non-Buddhists learn that Buddhism argues that there is no self, they are invariably confused. Such questions arise such as, "How can Buddhism assert there is no self when clearly I am conscious of my-self?" "How can Buddhism believe there is no self and yet have a doctrine of rebirth—that is, what is it exactly that moves from birth to death to birth again?" Let's address each of these questions and in so doing perhaps clarify what Buddhism means by "no-self."

To say one doesn't have a self seems contradictory; that is, don't I need a self to say there is no self? Someone familiar with the history of Western philosophy would recall Descartes' assertion, "Cogito Ergo Sum" (I think, therefore I am). To formulate a Buddhist answer to this question, we need to go back to the idea of "self."

Buddhism recognizes the difficulty with defining the "self" and actually offers its own attempt. Gautama asserted that the "self" is made up of five parts or aggregates, in Sanskrit, the five *skandhas*. The five skandhas are the form or body (rûpa), sensations (vedanâ), perceptions (*samjñâ*), mental formations (*samskâra*), and consciousness (vijñâna).[47]

Buddhism answers the question "What is the self?" with the proposal that the self is an aggregate of body, sensations, perceptions, mental formations, and consciousness. The idea that I am the sum of all my "parts" seems like a reasonable solution, and one with which many people might willingly agree. Gautama Buddha once compared the individual human life to a river:

> O Brâhmana, it is just like the mountain river, flowing far and swift, taking everything along with it; there is no moment, no instant, no second when it stops flowing, but it goes on flowing and continuing. So Brâhmana, is human life like a river.[48]

The Buddha goes on to state that each of these skandhas is impermanent and that this results in suffering, demonstrating how all three marks of existence are interconnected.

Many people would agree that the body is not permanent, but could one not claim that the body is not the self, and therefore there could still be a permanent self? One might argue, for example, that consciousness persists after death. In terms of this argument, it matters little whether one believes in heaven or in reincarnation—either way, consciousness could be said to continue after death.

Further, why did the Buddha say that the impermanence of the skandhas produces dukkha for the human person? In fact, his assertion was in the strongest possible form: "these five Aggregates together," he said, "which we popularly call a 'being', are *dukkha* itself."[49]

Of the five skandhas, body and sensations appear to be physical. We can acknowledge the impermanence of physical phenomena, and we can also acknowledge that their impermanence brings with it some degree of anxiety and dissatisfaction with this state of affairs. But what about the other three skandhas? Perceptions, mental formations, and consciousness are not physical. Perceptions and mental formations are actually part of consciousness, so perhaps that is where we should focus our examination—what is consciousness and how does it relate to dukkha?

Recall our discussion on the nature of consciousness in the section on the Four Noble Truths. Our ordinary consciousness, we said, bifurcates the world into subject and object, I and others. Ordinary consciousness is dualistic, that is, it divides the world into an inner awareness of myself as a subject and an outer awareness of things and other persons as objects. According to Japanese philosopher Keiji Nishitani, who was also trained in Western philosophy, "This standpoint of separation of subject and object, or opposition between within or without, is what we call the field of 'consciousness.'"[50] Consciousness as the fifth of the five aggregates simply *is* this underlying division between inner and outer, subject and object, self and others. Existence bears this same fundamental division, as existence is simply what consciousness is conscious of. The root of suffering is inherent in this dualistic structure of consciousness and existence: I can never fully know either self or other because it is impossible to look at the subject-I objectively and it is impossible to look at others and objects subjectively and still maintain my normal mode of consciousness. That can only happen when the ordinary structure of consciousness is sundered in the experience of Awakening.

Recall, however, that Buddhism teaches that all sentient beings have the Buddha nature. This Buddha nature is not the self posited by ordinary consciousness, but the genuine self or the selfless-self. No-self does not simply point to the impermanence of the self or the invisibility of the self, but most importantly (at least for Mahâyâna) it points to the nondual nature of both Truth and Reality. Highest truth is nondual, and therefore it is nonconceptual and unspeakable. Absolute reality is nondual, and therefore distinct selves and others do not exist there. The genuine self or the selfless-self transcends the ordinary consciousness of self to include both self and not-self.

In regard to the question of what transmigrates at death, the Buddhist could then argue it is the self (atman) that moves until its no-self (anatman) is realized in Awakening. Historically, one of the most important differences between Hinduism and Buddhism has been with respect to the notion of the atman. Hinduism teaches that the atman is permanent and that it is the same as Brahman, Atman-Brahman being the Self-Universe. Buddhism has argued for the nonpermanence of the self as distinct from the universe. The contention here is that the difference is a linguistic one rather than an existential one. For Buddhism, the ordinary self will continue to transmigrate until Awakening occurs whereupon the cycle ends:

> Faced with the mortal illness of the problematic self, the only cure is radical surgery. The *entire* dualistic consciousness must be uprooted and "replaced" with an Awakened consciousness that is not simply nondualistic but rather a nondualistic-dualistic consciousness, or, more succinctly rendered, a selfless self.[51]

This is the Mahâprajnâ (Great Wisdom) that a Buddhist expects to experience when he or she is finally Awakened. The time of Awakening is also the point when Mahâkarunâ (Great Compassion) comes into being. How does great compassion or love manifest as a result of Awakening?

The Buddhist Awakening results in a state of nonduality between self and other, where the one is truly seen as the other and the other as the self. When the reality of "I am I *and* I am not-I" or "I am I *and* I am the Universe" is experienced, the obstacle of egocentricity that taints all interpersonal relationships is extirpated and unobstructed compassion; regard for the other is lucidly manifest. This is the Buddhist understanding of Mahâkarunâ or love.

AHIMSA (NON-HARM)

Ahimsa is a Hindu, Jain, and Buddhist principle. It precludes the causing of suffering to any being, whether human or animal. The causing of any type of pain—psychological or financial as well as physical—is forbidden. The principle of ahimsa often, though not always, leads to the adoption of a vegetarian diet, or at least to the perception that that would be the ideal diet from a spiritual perspective. It also often leads to a refusal to engage in military combat or even in sports that intentionally hurt or kill animals.

You might be wondering what harm a little more harm could do, since Buddhists believe that life is already full of suffering. In the face of a life of suffering, why not espouse a "tough guy" attitude as the best way to cope? Buddhists believe that compassion and empathy are part of our original nature. They believe that no one harms another living being except out of hatred, greed, or ignorance. Hatred, greed, and ignorance disappear with Awakening, and our original nature, which is the Buddha nature, manifests in their stead. In other words, although Buddhists believe that suffering is ubiquitous, they do not believe that it is natural. We are not doomed to suffering and harm but capable of following a path (the Buddhist path) that leads to wisdom and compassion.

However, this line of reasoning leads to further questions. If Buddhists believe that our original nature is compassion and love, why are there Buddhist monks? Why do some Buddhists avoid romantic and family attachments? Are not monks choosing lives of dispassion rather than compassion?

NONATTACHMENT

Buddhists believe that what we normally call love is really attachment. In its grossest form, it is attachment to pleasure, the pleasure of being with and enjoying a sexual or romantic partner. In its subtler forms, it is attachment to a parent, a child, a spouse, or a friend. As our ordinary way of referring to such relationships reveals, they are more a matter of emotional dependence and social status than they are a matter of altruistic compassion. Such relationships form a "larger self" but only to the extent that the participants think in terms of "us" versus "you" rather than in terms of "I" versus "you." Even more revealing is the fact that we speak of "*having* a friend," "*having* a wife (or husband)," "*having* children," and even "*having* sex." When we are dependent on something or someone, we want to "have" it, that is, to control or possess it. When we love someone without ego involvement, we want to free that person rather than control her or him. Buddhist compassion is a matter of liberating others, not forming dependent relationships with them. The monastic lifestyle, rightly lived, is a matter of freedom from such attachments.

However, a householder can be further along the Buddhist path and closer to nirvana than someone who lives in a monastery. That is because real relationships don't work very well when they are a matter of attachments and dependencies. The relationship itself can be a guide to freeing love rather than attached love, to genuine overcoming of dualistic thought and action rather than a furthering of our tendency to want to grasp at things and persons and "have" them.

As in all religions that have both monastic and family lifestyles, the monastics embody the principle of liberation from the ordinary, deluded ways of the world, while those who live in the world without succumbing to its ways embody the nonduality of freedom from the world and compassionate commitment to it.

TIBETAN BUDDHIST VIEW OF TRANSMIGRATION AT DEATH

You may have heard of *The Tibetan Book of the Dead*. It has been available in translation in the West for several decades and was a popular book on college campuses in the 1960s. This book describes what happens when a person dies, according to Tibetan Buddhism. Because the book serves as a manual to assist in both the process of living and the process of dying, Sogyal Rinpoche has called it the "Tibetan Book of Living and Dying."[52]

I close this chapter with *The Tibetan Book of the Dead* because it provides an example of how Buddhist teachings and Buddhist beliefs about karma and rebirth are applied at this important time in a person's life. It provides an example of how the Buddhist worldview works in practice.

The book describes the stages of the dying process. Even as one is dying, a certain consciousness is still active. Therefore, we experience different things at each stage. Tibetan Buddhist scholar Robert Thurman presents the eight stages of death in this fashion:

THE STAGES OF DEATH: DISSOLUTION AND EXPERIENCES [53]	
DISSOLUTION	EXPERIENCE
1. earth to water	mirage
2. water to fire	smokiness
3. fire to wind	fireflies in the sky
4. wind to consciousness	clear candle flame
5. gross consciousness to luminance	clear moonlit sky
6. luminance to radiance	clear sunlit sky
7. radiance to imminence	clear pitch-darkness
8. imminence to translucency	clear light of clear predawn sky

THE TIBETAN ART OF DYING

The Tibetan Book of the Dead describes what the transmigrating self experiences postmortem. As Robert Thurman notes, this text is known in Tibet as *The Great Book of Natural Liberation through Understanding in the Between*. It provides guidance to help people deal with the death of others close to them. It is, in a sense, a map of human dying and death.

To use the book as it is designed to be used one needs to be a believer and to work under the guidance of a qualified teacher. However, for our purposes we can examine the book as an argument for a certain view of death. The book attempts to provide its readers with a clear view of what happens when one dies and how one should prepare for the inevitableness of death.

According to Thurman, the book argues for two levels of preparation for death: ordinary and extraordinary. We will deal only with ordinary preparation here. Ordinary preparation can be subdivided into five areas of preparation: informational, imaginational, ethical, meditational, and intellectual.

Informational means to inform oneself about the interior physical aspects of death by studying the Tibetan (and Western scientific) views of what happens when one dies. Imaginational means to use one's imaginative powers to visualize death and positive realities such as parinirvâṇâ. Asian art and story are replete with examples of positive realms that one might encounter after death. One should study the sutras that describe these lands of bliss or, if one is a Westerner, one can read of the visions of the mystics in such traditions as Christianity, Judaism, or Islam for guidance.

According to Thurman, the most important ethical practices are generosity, compassion, and tolerance. It is also important to infuse one's life with an awareness of the transitoriness of life; this will temper one's greed, selfishness, and tension.

Meditational preparation involves doing contemplative practices that induce calm, fire the imagination, generate loving-kindness, and stimulate mindfulness. It is important to note that these preparations are not anti-intellectual but rather are supported by one's intellectual interest and drive to understand.

For the components of extraordinary preparation, the interested reader is encouraged to consult Thurman's book (*The Tibetan Book of the Dead*, Bantam Doubleday Dell, 1994) and others that relate to the Tibetan art of dying.

The purpose of *The Tibetan Book of the Dead* and several other Vajrayâna Buddhist practices is to enable the dying person to retain lucidity and recognize the various stages as he or she progresses through them. Although one's physical body moves into death at stage four, one's consciousness persists. Consequently, the dying person is able to continue to benefit from his or her practice and instruction while alive. He or she can also benefit from oral instructions provided by a trained teacher who sits with the dying person. Robert Thurman writes:

> The meditative practices associated with between-state training are crucial for sharpening attention so you can become aware of the process, slow down the transitions, and remain lucidly aware of the changes as they occur.[54]

The goal of *The Tibetan Book of the Dead* is to bring the dying person into Awakening and not have him or her transmigrate into a new life.

If one has been trained properly and has the guidance of a trained lama, one may still gain release from samsara even postmortem. If not able to gain this eleventh-hour release, then one moves into the next life.

Tibetan Buddhists use this book to prepare for the experience of death. Rather than fearing death, they want to use the dying experience to consolidate their spiritual prowess so that Awakening will ensue. *The Tibetan Book of the Dead* is a fascinating treatise that challenges the dominant Western view of what happens when we die.

5

Worship

In a quiet and untrammeled spot the practitioner
should resplendently arrange a single chamber
to use as the ritual sanctuary [daochang]....
A fine altar-piece should be installed in the sanctuary
and on it placed a single copy of the Lotus Sūtra.
There is no need to enshrine any
other images, relics, or scriptures.

—From *Fahna sanmei chanyi*,
ed. Junjirō Takakusu and Watanabe Kaigyoku,
Tokyo: Taisho issai-kyō kankō-kai,
1914–1922, no. 1941: 949–954, vol. 46.

A Buddhist place of worship is called a temple. Most of the large temples built in one of the classical architectural styles are located in Asia, but there are Buddhist temples all over the world, including in major metropolitan areas in the United States and Europe. Wherever you live, you are most likely within a few hours of a Buddhist place of worship.

Simply because Buddhist temples are found everywhere, it is difficult to generalize about their appearance, furnishings, and services. That said, there are some elements that appear in most Buddhist temples. In the following section, I will describe some of those common characteristics. Later in this chapter I will describe some specific temples in Japan and in the United States.

THE STRUCTURE OF A BUDDHIST TEMPLE
The Temple Complex

The Buddhist temple has historically been not only a place of worship but also a center for learning, healing, and celebrations. Not infrequently it also served as a monastic residence (a monastery). The monks, as custodians of society's knowledge, doled out what was often the only type of medical help available. Because a Buddhist temple fulfills many purposes, it is almost invariably a set of buildings located on a large parcel of land. In other words, temples are not usually single buildings but an entire complex of structures and the land on which they are located (the temple grounds).

Most Buddhist temples have an entrance gate that provides access to the temple grounds. However, in smaller temples with only a single building, this may not be the case. There will be a sign in front indicating the name of the temple and perhaps its school or affiliation.

Two buildings commonly found on the temple grounds are the main hall and a lecture hall. The main hall contains objects used in worship, such as statues. Lecture halls may also display objects of worship, but their primary purpose is to serve as the site for meetings and lectures.

Upon entering the main hall, the worshipper may be asked to remove his or her shoes. If so, it will be clearly evident that this is the expectation. The purpose of shoe removal is to maintain the cleanliness or purity of the temple. It is also easier to sit in prayer or meditation if one is not wearing shoes. A third reason for removal of shoes is to protect the sometimes fragile materials used in the construction of the worship space. For example, the straw mats (Jp.: tatami) used for flooring in Japanese temples are easily damaged by shoes.

Buddhist Altars

Every worship space has at least one altar present somewhere in the room. There may be several altars in one room or in several different buildings, if the temple is a compound made up of several buildings.

Buddhist altars vary greatly in design, but one will usually find some representation of a Buddha or bodhisattva, perhaps represented in a statue, painting, scroll, etc. The Buddhist figure represented may indicate with which sect of Buddhism the temple is associated. For example, in a Pure Land temple a representation of Amida Buddha will be on the main altar.

Often there is a main altar flanked by side altars on either side. The side altars will be smaller, but they will also contain a Buddhist figure, perhaps a Buddha, bodhisattva, or the founder of the sect.

Candles or incense are customarily placed on the altar or in the area around it. In some cases, the worshipper is invited to light the candles or incense. There may be a small coin box present, in which case the worshipper may put a coin in, take a candle or stick of incense, and place it in the appropriate place. The incense might be placed in an incense burner that, when filled with burning sticks, gives rise to a cloud that fills the air.

The altar and its contents are usually made of natural materials, such as wood or metals. The altar may include candles or candelabras that are lit and maintained by the devotees who live at the temple. Fruit, flowers, or other objects that have been donated to the temple by believers will be placed on the altar. One may also find prayers, fortunes, portions of sutras, and other instructional material near the altar.

Temple Art

In many temples, the visitor finds artistic representations intended for pedagogical or instructional purposes. These may include paintings, quotations, and even gardens, such as the famous rock gardens associated with certain Japanese Zen Buddhist temples.

Vajrayâna temples often have prayer wheels. These are cylindrical drums that have prayers written on them. When a believer spins the prayer wheel with his or her hands, the prayer is symbolically sent to the wind and so out into the world to benefit others. Sometimes there will be a long row of prayer wheels, enabling the worshipper to walk down the path and spin many prayer wheels in a very short amount of time.

Temple Visitors and Residents

Of course, when one visits a Buddhist temple, one also will see Buddhist practitioners, both lay and monastic. The layperson may be there for individual prayer or meditation, to attend a regularly scheduled service, or perhaps for a special service or ceremony that was arranged on his or her behalf. Examples of special services would be a birth ceremony, a wedding, a funeral, or a commemoration on the anniversary of a death.

Often a believer will pause in prayer before the altar. He or she may intone a set prayer or devise one of his or her own. The believer may also choose to chant a mantra or sutra before the altar. Many Buddhists employ a rosary (Skt.: *mala*), which is a set of prayer beads. A rosary will often have 108 beads (representing the 108 human passions or worldly desires). It should be noted, however, that rosaries do differ in number of beads and in the materials of which they are made.

Monks or nuns are present to take care of the temple, to preside over the ceremonies, and to provide other services to laypersons.

In return for these services, laypersons donate time and money to the temple for its upkeep and expenses. Many Buddhist temples are also monasteries, but not all Buddhist temples have monks or nuns who live in the temple.

Other Items Found in Temples

The lotus is a common Buddhist symbol. Within a temple, a statue of the Buddha or a bodhisattva might be sitting or standing on a lotus. The lotus usually symbolizes purity. The lotus plant grows in water; the leaves extend out of the water and so are not touched by any dirt in the water. The lotus symbolizes the Buddhist practitioner, who is in the world but also untouched—unsullied by the world. In some Buddhist interpretations, the lotus is a symbol of the feminine principle or the female sex organ.

The temples of Tibetan Buddhist sects, and also of esoteric sects in China and Japan, might contain a vajra. The vajra is a thunderbolt-like symbol that may appear in pictures or be cast in metal. The vajra is a symbol of the knowledge and power needed to overcome spiritual ignorance and bad thoughts. It sometimes symbolizes the male sex organ and in such cases it might accompany the lotus.

Very often a bell will be found at a Buddhist temple. In Japan, you may find a separate belfry with a bell so large that a large log on a chain is used as the clapper. These bells were used for time keeping, in ceremonies, and for maintaining the daily schedule of the temple.

The wheel is a common symbol of Buddhism. It represents Buddhist teaching, which may be referred to as "the turning of the wheel of the law (dharma)." Other items that might be found at a Buddhist temple include vases, mirrors, books of Buddhist sutras, and a reliquary known as a *stûpa*.

A stûpa is a dome-shaped structure that may be quite large or quite small. It is a symbolic burial mound; in ancient India the cremated remains of great kings were enshrined in stûpas. In some cases, Buddhist stûpas may actually contain a relic of

Gautama Buddha, such as a lock of hair or a tooth. Whether they contain an actual relic or not, stûpas are sites where offerings and devotions take place.

A BUDDHIST TEMPLE IN JAPAN

There are thousands of temples in Japan, ranging from large temple complexes to smaller, single edifices. Indeed, even a single large city, like Kyoto, may have several thousand temples, while almost every smaller city has at least one temple.

One of the most-visited Buddhist temples in the world, Todaiji is a temple of the Kegon sect of Buddhism. It is most famed for the great statue of the Buddha that resides in what is said to be the world's largest wooden building, the Great Buddha Hall. Originally built in the eighth century C.E., the building was burned twice (1180, 1567) as well as being reconstructed in the early eighteenth century.

Visitors to Todaiji are struck by the presence of people and of deer. The park where the temple is located is called Deer Park (in recognition of Deer Park at Sârnâth, the location of Gautama Buddha's first sermon) and deer freely amble around begging food from the tourists and pilgrims. The popular temples in Japan also have a large number of stalls lining the paths, where merchants sell everything from film, toys, and postcards to Buddhist articles.

The entrance to Todaiji is through the great south gate (Daimon) that permits passage into the sacred space within. Two enormous guardians stand on either side of the gate protecting all within from evil spirits.

Once through the gate, the pilgrim approaches the inner temple through a side door that requires an admission fee. The popular temples in Japan frequently charge an admission fee to help cover their costs. Stepping through the side door, one is immediately struck by the size of the large temple building that houses the great Buddha, the Daibutsu.

An immense incense urn, consistent with the scale of the temple building, stands in the middle of the path close to the temizuya, the purification basin that pilgrims and tourists alike use to ritually purify themselves before approaching the altar. After the optional purchase of an incense stick, the pilgrim ascends the great staircase of the main hall.

To the right of the massive doorway stands a weathered Yakushi, a so-called Medicine Buddha. Petitioners approach to ask for healing. The person generally places a few coins in the coinbox at the base of the altar, touches the part of the seated statue that corresponds to the part of his or her own body that requires healing, and ties a mikuji (fortune) on the banister behind them.

Stepping over the threshold into the main hall, one is immediately struck by the immensity of the Buddha figure who rises up out of the dim light. The Daibutsu, ordered by Emperor Shômu to be constructed in 743, is a representation of Vairocana Buddha. The casting of the statue actually began early in 747 and was finally dedicated on April 9, 752. Work continued even after this on the statue's pedestal and aureole (ring of light, halo). One of the devotional pictures that one can buy at Todaiji states that "more than ten thousand priests and musicians from India, China and Korea as well as Japan" attended the dedication.

The Rushana (Vairocana) Daibutsu is a Japanese National Treasure standing forty-nine feet in height. It required five hundred tons of copper to construct. Two other statues, smaller but still immense, flank the main altar.

Although Todaiji is obviously unique in many ways, it appropriately serves as our example of a Japanese Buddhist temple. More Japanese Buddhists visit this temple than visit local neighborhood temples. In addition, this early Buddhist temple in Japan includes all the elements that one can see in considerably smaller temples all over Asia.

A BUDDHIST TEMPLE IN THE UNITED STATES

Buddhist places of worship can be found throughout the United States and Europe, increasingly not only in urban settings but also in rural areas. There is not a major city in the West without several Buddhist centers representing different Asian Buddhist

TIBETAN MONASTERIES

In his recent book, *The Sound of Two Hands Clapping*, Georges Dreyfus provides a wonderfully insightful look inside Tibetan monasticism. Currently a Professor of Religion at Williams College, Dreyfus spent many years as a Tibetan Buddhist monk.

Dreyfus describes the Tibetan monastery as one centered on rituals regardless of whether the monastery community is made up of a handful or thousands of monks. He describes his own efforts to memorize the ritual manual that guided practice within the temple. The routine of ritual inside Dre-pung Monastery during debate sessions included a morning service, then a brief prayer in the courtyard. Following a debate, another service ensued, another courtyard prayer, and then another debate. In the afternoon, there may be yet another debate and then the main ritual of the day: the prayer of the evening debate. This last ritual contained more than fifty prayers and lasted more than two hours, Dreyfus reports. (44)

The rituals are usually performed in the assembly hall, which is particularly valued for this reason and also because it is the location where the monks receive support (food, money) from their sponsors. One could draw a parallel with a Christian chapel, which is likewise the site where important rituals occur and the place where the church receives offerings from its parishioners.

Beyond the daily rituals, the temple is busy with rituals prescribed by the Vinaya Pitaka and with the Buddhist holy days, e.g., the commemoration of the Buddha's Awakening. Temples will also celebrate school-specific rituals (those related to a particular "school" or type of Buddhism) as well as temple-specific rituals (e.g., the celebration of the foundation day of the temple).

Dreyfus describes rituals called "foot firming," which are performed for supporters of the temple. This type of ritual may be done for a variety of different purposes, such as healing or repelling evil spirits. The timing of these rituals is either astrologically determined or determined by a diviner. Monks, individuals, corporations, or governments can request such rituals, and the monks may come to depend on these rituals as an essential part of their support.

A local monastery operates as we have described. A central monastery has additional functions because it serves as a training center for monks. However, whether the monastery is local or central, all of monastic life centers on rituals.

sects. Large numbers of Americans now live within easy driving distance of a Vietnamese Buddhist temple that is the social center of an immigrant community; a Zen temple largely peopled by thirty-something Caucasian Americans; or a meeting of Sôka Gakkai Buddhists, a form of Buddhism with a strong following in the African American community. Buddhist temples in the United States range from large, dedicated buildings to residential homes that have been converted to a weekly gathering place for prayer. In short, Buddhist temples are no longer filled solely with Asians.

The American Buddhist temple that we will focus on is located in a house in a residential neighborhood in a city in the Midwest. It has been in existence for about twenty-five years and is affiliated with a larger network of temples that originated with an esteemed Japanese Zen teacher who came to the United States in the 1950s and established a home temple. One of his students, a fifty-year-old American-born male, who first became interested in Zen Buddhism in the 1960s, was sanctioned by this master as his dharma heir and empowered to teach at and then run this subtemple. Within the national network of temples founded by the original Japanese Zen teacher, we see a second generation of teachers, the dharma heirs of the original set of students, moving into positions of leadership.

The temple is set up as a nonprofit organization. It has an attractive Web site that provides meditation schedules, announces special events, posts newsletters, etc. Each weekend offers an opportunity to learn how to meditate so that one may feel more at ease in participating in the daily practice or the weekly session (offered on a Sunday morning). The Zen Center also offers opportunities for families to be involved in practice and other support activities. There are several retreats (sesshin) per year, open to both members and nonmembers (membership often requires a small, yearly fee). Sesshin may be held in the city temple or outside the city in a rural temple. The temple is growing very slowly and financially it is, at best, a break-even affair. Sources of revenue include the memberships, selling of tapes and books, and donations from members and friends of the temple. Some larger annual gifts help as well.

PRACTICE IN A BUDDHIST CENTER

The number and type of practice sessions provided by a Buddhist temple depend upon its location and the type of Buddhism it represents. In this section, we will look at the practice schedule in an American Zen Center.

The "Clouds in Water Zen Center" is located in downtown St. Paul, Minnesota. It has been in existence for about a decade. The home page of their Web site states, "We are a dharma center that offers intensive Zen training in practice-realization that this very life is a 'field of boundless emptiness from the beginning.' We offer many gateways to Buddhist practice and welcome all who seek clear wisdom and radiant compassion." [55]

One can register for classes on-line and donate money to the Center on-line. The News and Updates section indicated a busy schedule at the beginning of 2004, with a fifteen-week program on the teachings of the Buddha and making peace, the visit of a noted Zen scholar for several lectures with zazen practice, numerous classes, and a notice that an article on the Center's children and youth practice program had appeared in the St. Paul newspaper.

The "Sunday Morning Meditation" schedule is as follows:

8:00–8:45	Compassion Practice
9:00	First meditation period, fifteen minutes
9:15	Second meditation period, sitting or walking meditation
9:30	Dharma talk by either our guiding teacher or a guest teacher, or a student talk by a senior student
10:30	Tea and conversation in our social hall [56]

Sunday worship is open to anyone and instructions on how to meditate consistent with the Center's practice are made available either at the Center or on-line. Daily meditation is offered at the

Center on Mondays through Thursdays with sitting starting at 5:30 A.M. and ending with a liturgy from 6:50 to 7:05. There are also noontime, evening, Tuesday afternoon, and Saturday morning practice schedules.

The "Compassion Practice" mentioned in the Sunday Morning Meditation schedule is a special practice that lasts for a hundred days. It is "the practice of invoking compassionate energy for those close to us and for the world through chanting the 'Ten Line Kannon Sutra of Timeless Life.'"[57] Cards are filled with joys or concerns that are read during the service.

LEARNING ABOUT BUDDHIST PRACTICE

Tricycle: The Buddhist Review, a popular magazine on Buddhist practice, lists many opportunities to study Buddhism. The list includes speaking tours of esteemed Buddhist teachers, retreats, visits to monasteries, and a classified listing of Dharma Centers. Both domestic and international opportunities are available. A simple Internet search will provide additional information about Buddhist places and practices.

Today, one can travel to historic Buddhist sites in Asia as a tourist or pilgrim and in a matter of days see sites that not too long ago no one person had collectively ever seen. Many Buddhist sutras have been translated into English and some are even available on-line. In today's world, opportunities to explore the many dimensions of Buddhist practice abound.

6

Growing Up Buddhist

A child is innocent but lacks the maturity
and the wisdom to handle his own life.
Adults have the maturity to some extent,
but lack the innocence.
This innocence bestows wisdom,
it can only be achieved through the practice
of "direct seeing" into one's own mind.

—Dr. Thynn Thynn, "Children's Direct Seeing,"
Sakyadhita Newsletter, 1994, vol. 5, no. 1.

The Buddhist temple historically has occupied a central role in Buddhist societies. As we learned in the last chapter, it served as a center of learning, study, healing, guidance, work, celebration, and mourning. Today, young men in some Southeast Asian countries continue to depend upon the temple and monasticism to supply an important part of their formal education. In some areas, a young man is not deemed ready for marriage until he has received this type of education.

Lay Buddhists continue to rely upon the monks and their understanding of herbal medicine for medical treatment, and this is oftentimes the only medical treatment available. They visit the temple to pray, socialize, and confer with the monks and nuns who support the spiritual and psychological health of the community-at-large. And, certainly, over the course of their lifetimes there will be many visits to the Buddhist temple to attend rituals of celebration and mourning. The myriad ways in which Buddhism intersects the lives of its believers are often specific to certain countries, towns, and even temples, but a few examples may serve to illustrate how Buddhism impresses itself upon the lives of its followers.

THE BUDDHIST FAMILY

In rebirth, a person is born into this world with a karmic legacy derived from past lives. Buddhist parents are also connected to preconception as they might have offered petitionary prayers: They may have prayed for the ability to conceive, or asked that their baby might be a boy, healthy, and so forth. Even prior to that, prayers had likely been offered as each prospective partner sought another person with whom to raise a family!

The Buddhist Family in Japan

As we consider Japanese Buddhist families, we need to keep in mind that Shinto is the other major tradition in Japan and that it also plays a significant role in rites of passage. For example, the baby's first visit to a Shinto shrine after birth (Jp.: Miyamairi) is a cause for celebration, as are the traditional visits to the shrine of children who are seven, five, and three years old. In Japan this is known as the Shichi-go-san festival, from the Japanese words for "seven" (shichi), "five" (go), and "three" (san). The relationship between Shinto and Buddhism in Japan is syncretistic, as is evident in the fact that even as people pray for protection of their children at a Shinto shrine they simultaneously look to a Buddhist temple for the same reason.

Japanese children of school age may seek out spiritual assistance at the family temple in preparation for a critical exam or as an aid in social relationships. Occasionally, a Buddhist priest is sought out for advice in raising a child or to perform a ritual for a special purpose, such as for healing. Special rituals may be solicited by grandparents as well as parents. The traditional Asian household contains three generations, and it is very often the grandparents that encourage and lead the religious practices of the family.

As the child comes of age, his or her visits to the temple may be focused on securing a promising job or a spouse. Marriages themselves are most often conducted by a Shinto priest. However, as the couple has children, cares for their aging parents, and in turn age themselves, the practical application of Buddhism to every aspect of the lifespan continues. Prayers, devotions, and other Buddhist practices assist in achieving goals and in maintaining well-being at every age.

As happens in every religious tradition, there are those who do not seem to have much faith in the prayers recited on the temple grounds, demonstrating at best an "it can only help" attitude toward their devotions. There are also, of course, many genuinely devout Buddhists in Japan and in other Buddhists countries.

In many Buddhist temples in Japan, one may purchase amulets. These are thought to protect the believer from various concerns such as fire, specific illnesses, pregnancy (or infertility), failure of entrance exams, or business failure. Certain temples are renowned for being particularly efficacious in protecting the believer from one or another of these concerns, and people will travel great distances to visit these temples and benefit from their famed power.

Fuda (flat pieces of inscribed wood) and omamori (small cloth brocade bags with an inscription) are the most common types of protective amulets available in Japanese Buddhist temples. Train or bus companies will often place these items on their trains or buses to protect passengers from an accident. The household, too, may have its own omamori to protect it from fire or intruders. Similar practices are found in other Buddhist countries. Indeed, the popularity of such practices helps Buddhism to retain its relevance in the day-to-day life of believers. It should be noted, however, that many of these practices originated with the indigenous traditions in the country and predated the transmission of Buddhism to that country.

The Buddhist Family in Myanmar (Burma)

In Myanmar (formerly called Burma), Theravâda is the dominant form of Buddhism. About eighty-eight percent of the population is Buddhist. The majority of these are very devout, and the Buddhist temple is almost invariably the center of village life.

In a short essay entitled "A Buddhist Family in Burma," U Kin Maung[58] describes how his own family practices Buddhism:

> From his childhood, a Buddhist is taught to respect Buddha, Dhamma, Sangha, his parents and Teachers. During the month of Thadingyut, which marks the end of the Buddhist lent, young persons would approach their parents and Teachers to pay their respects by bowing down deeply before them and receive their blessings, while fruits, tinned provisions, candles and other such articles are placed before them as token for their respect.[59]

Upon rising in the morning, his children bow before the family shrine that is on the south side of the house (south and east are the preferred directions). As is the case in Buddhist families across Asia, Maung's live-in mother-in-law is the person primarily responsible for household practice and maintenance of the shrine. In front of the numerous Buddhist statues that have been collected are "three goblets filled with seasonal flowers, little silver cups and plates for offerings of food and water, which are really a symbolic gesture on our part as if Buddha were alive and with us."[60] Maung's mother-in-law also meets the monks who visit the home as part of their daily rounds to collect alms and provides them with small amounts of food.

The entire family will pray at the home shrine each morning, intoning the Three Refuges and the Five Precepts. Laypersons ordinarily follow only the Five Precepts, but they may increase the number of precepts they follow during certain times of the year. The entire family visits the monastery and pagodas often. They usually bring food and have a family picnic there. The monks meet the children and provide them with plantains or sweets.

At the end of the day, the children will pray before the family shrine. Usually the parents will be present to listen to the prayers of their children.

JIZÔ BOSATSU: A BUDDHIST DEITY FOR CHILDREN

Jizô Bosatsu (Skt.: Ksitigarbha) plays an important role in Japanese society. Inarguably, the most commonly encountered bodhisattva image in Japan is his. You may see him standing by himself on a busy street corner, on a playground, or in a cemetery; or you may see great numbers of Jizô statues standing side-by-side in a virtual pyramid of statues.

Jizô means "He who encompasses the earth." Bosatsu is the Japanese word for bodhisattva. Jizô Bosatsu appeared early in Mahâyâna history in India but didn't become popular until coming to China—where he is known as *Dizang*—in the fifth century C.E.

Dizang's myth is related in a sutra named after him. Prior to becoming a bodhisattva, he was a young Brahmin girl who vowed to save all beings from the torments of hell. Although Jizô works to help beings in all of the Six Realms of Existence (those in hell, hungry ghosts, animals, demons, humans, and deities), he is especially determined to aid those in hell:

> In hell, his mission is to lighten the burden caused by previous evil actions, to secure from the judges of hell an alleviation of the fate of the condemned and to console them. Thus in the popular mind, Ksitigarbha has become the Bodhisattva of hells *par excellence.*[61]

Jizô is the guardian of children who are stillborn, lost through miscarriage, or aborted. Children who die prematurely are believed to go to the underworld, which is a place of suffering. Jizô works to lessen the intensity and duration of their suffering. Little heaps of stones around Jizô statues reflect the belief that a stone offered in faith by a parent will reduce the amount of time his or her child spends in hell. (In Hinduism and Buddhism, hell is not a place of eternal punishment. As soon as one's negative karma is used up, one is released to enter one of the other realms of existence.)

A Japanese story about Jizô locates him in hell, "on a sandy beach called Sai-no-Kawara, [where] dead infants spend their time building votive structures with small pebbles to increase their merits and those of their parents. But every evening, demons, especially an old woman named Sôzu-no-Kawara no Uba, demolish their work. Ksitigarbha then consoles the unhappy children, telling them, 'In this land of shades, I am your father and your mother: trust me morning and evening.'"[62]

Sometimes grieving mothers will take a dead child's tiny garments and dress a Jizô statue in them, hoping that the gift will result in special protection for their child. A tiny hat or bib on a Jizô statue, on the other hand, is usually the gift of a rejoicing mother whose child was healed after she prayed to Jizô.

Jizô may be known by different names, depending upon which of his powers is being invoked. For example, Taue Jizô helps farmers to plant rice, while Koyasu Jizô, who in a feminine form is considered as a "bestower of children,"[63] protects children and helps ease childbirth. Enmei Jizô Bosatsu serves as a "celestial babysitter"; fieldworkers will leave their children playing in the vicinity of this Jizô while they work.

In modern Japan, Jizô's most important function is to offer aid in the event of a mizuko (literally "water baby"), an aborted or stillborn child. Japan has a high abortion rate, and Jizô helps both the parents and the aborted fetus, both here and in the next life. Some Buddhist temples have developed rituals to avert the suffering resulting from an ignoble death so that the aborted or stillborn fetus does not need to endure that agony.[64]

BUDDHISM AND DEATH IN JAPAN

At the time of a death, Buddhism takes center stage in the life of a Japanese family. Ian Reader, a scholar of Japanese religions, reports that a 1984 survey found that of the more than eighteen hundred people who were asked the reasons they would visit their temple and consult a Buddhist priest, seventy-eight percent of the respondents indicated they would do so for reasons connected to funerals, whereas only eight percent would do so for "spiritual reasons." The remaining fourteen percent gave no response.[65]

As Shinto has become connected with marriage in Japan, Buddhism has become connected with funerals. All the Buddhists sects in Japan have developed mortuary rituals, and it seems that the primary function of Buddhism in the eyes of the Japanese populace is to carry out these rituals. Buddhism assumed this role almost from the beginning of its presence in Japan in the sixth century. An imperial edict in C.E. 685 decreed that all households should have a butsudan (Buddhist altar) to venerate the ancestors of the family. The first cremation of a Buddhist monk took place in 700 and members of the Imperial family were thereafter cremated.[66]

Japanese Buddhism found its niche relative to Shinto by articulating a view of the afterlife, something that Shinto did not offer. Shinto did encourage veneration of the ancestors, however, and Buddhism adopted the practice of ancestor veneration. This was an accommodation on the part of Buddhism, since its doctrines of rebirth and no-self should have precluded the possibility of an enduring individual person after death. Yet Buddhism in Japan acknowledged an enduring spirit after death that needed to be venerated by the living.

The mixing of Shinto and Buddhist beliefs and practices persists in modern Japan. It bewilders the observer of Japanese religiosity and sometimes it confuses the Japanese people themselves:

> It was the apparent spiritual and magical powers accumulated by those who trained in the Buddhist tradition, aligned to the powers possessed by Buddhism in the form of its Buddha figures, statues, prayers, incantations and rituals, that were responsible for convincing the Japanese that Buddhism had the ability to transform the spirits of the dead and lead them to enlightenment after death, thereby eradicating the impurities and pollutions associated with death.[67]

The above quotation makes reference to "the impurities and pollutions associated with death." The idea that death is a source of pollution is an ancient and powerful aspect of Japanese culture. It is for this very reason that Shinto priests do not conduct funerals, leaving this polluting work to the Buddhists. The emphasis on purity is evident in the Japanese fondness for onsen (hot springs) and sento (public baths), and in the multiple uses of salt as a purifier, including inside the sumo ring. The connection between death and impurity is underscored in the ancient Japanese myths, which describe how the male partner of Japan's founding couple, Izanagi, ritually cleansed himself in order to remove the pollutants that he had come in contact with as a result of his descent into the underworld.

Although funeral observances vary from region to region, we can offer a general portrayal of what happens at the time of a death.[68] As occurred in the West, funerals in Japan are transitioning from being largely home affairs to being funeral-home experiences. But, as of today, the home continues to be an important setting.

Upon death, the body is washed either at home or in the hospital and the orifices are stuffed with cotton. The body is then dressed and taken to where the service will be held, usually in the deceased's home temple. In modern Japan, it is not always readily apparent which temple should be contacted, because people relocate more often now than they did previously.

Once the proper temple has been determined, its priest is contacted by whomever is overseeing the details of the funeral service, whether that be the mortuary or a family member. Traditionally, the eldest son decides on the day of the funeral, the setting of the altar, the food that will be served, and so on.

The body is placed on dry ice, either before the family altar at home or in the mortuary hall. A family member remains with the body until it is placed in a coffin. When placed in the coffin, the body is dressed in white, the Buddhist color signifying death. Paper money is placed in the coffin, "for the deceased to pay for the toll across the River of the Three Hells,"[69] along with other items that the deceased may have enjoyed in life.

When the actual service commences, a white tent is erected outside the door of the home. This serves the dual purpose of indicating the location to arriving mourners, and informing passersby and neighboring residents that a death has occurred.

A table is set up with a registry in which guests will sign their names. Mourners may also place condolence money (koden) for the family in a special envelope. The amount of money is indicated on the outside of the envelope and varies depending on the relation of the mourner to the deceased and other factors. The amount of money that is received is recorded in the registry that will be given to the family later.

As one enters the room where the body is laid to rest, one is greeted by the smell of incense. Buddhism utilizes incense in many of its rituals; in funerals it is used because of its purifying effects. New arrivals stand or sit before the body and the altar; they bow, utter a prayer, ring a bell, and place a pinch of incense in the already smoldering pile of loose incense. The family members are present, and greetings and condolences are shared with each person at this time.

When the priest arrives, he speaks with the family and then begins the wake with a sutra reading. As he reads, the family members, in hierarchal order, bow, offer incense, and return to their seats. Then all the participants do the same in turn. When the sutra reading is finished, everyone bows and the wake is over. A small present from the family is given to each person as he or she leaves. Depending on their relation to the family, some people will only attend the wake and not the funeral.

The funeral is often the next day (the Japanese have not traditionally practiced embalming). It will be held at the temple, and the body is placed before an altar that the mortuary has created for the occasion. A wooden tablet with the death name (kaimyo) of the deceased is set up. This tablet is called an ihai. The death name has been given to the deceased by the priest and recorded in the temple registry.

As at the wake, the priest intones an appropriate sutra as the mourners take their turns coming forward individually. Upon conclusion of the sutra reading, the priest leaves the room. A representative of the family, the eldest son if possible, gets up and thanks everyone for attending the service. Those who were not able to attend will often be represented by the reading of letters that were sent to the family. The coffin that has been open to this point is now sealed.

As everyone stands, the pallbearers carry the coffin out of the temple and to the hearse. In Japan, the hearse is designed to look like a temple on wheels. It conveys the body to the crematorium with the family members following.

At the crematorium, the coffin is placed on a sliding tray that will move into the crematory oven. The family watches as the coffin moves into the oven. They are told when they can return to pick up the remains. The family returns home or to the funeral hall, sometimes by a different route than the one they used in coming, so as to not have the deceased spirit follow them. They wait until the appointed time whereupon they return to the crematorium. There the cremated body is displayed for the family and each member is provided special hashi (chopsticks). With these hashi, the bones of the deceased are to be picked up and placed in the urn. An attendant is present to assist. Each bone is picked up by two members of the family at the same time (this is why you will never see two Japanese people pick up food at the same time when eating—this is only done at funerals). It is particularly important to find the Adam's apple and place it in the urn.

Upon completion of this task, the urn is covered and wrapped in a white cloth. The urn will be placed on the family altar in the home for a period of time. Ultimately, the urn or parts of the remains are placed at a family grave site and regular memorial services are held thereafter at determined intervals.

In all Buddhist sects, the time period immediately following physical death is considered very important. The Tibetan Buddhist tradition in particular has paid considerable attention to this period of time, and it is the subject of *The Tibetan Book of the Dead.*

Across the Buddhist world, similar death rituals are performed. The preparation of the body, the reciting of sutras, and cremation will be carried out as we have described; whether the funeral takes place in Thailand, China, or Sri Lanka.

BUDDHIST MONASTICISM

As one visits a Buddhist temple throughout the world, he or she may encounter a monk or nun praying, chanting, selling religious items, or sweeping a walk. One may rightly wonder, "How does one become a Buddhist monk or nun and how do they live their lives?"

As you may recall, the early canonical doctrines that pertained to being a monk or nun appeared in the Vinaya Pitika. This document still lies at the heart of monastic practice; although over time it has been transformed and reinterpreted.

The early Buddhist monastics were organized into districts. Each district had an observance hall (uposatha) that served as a gathering place for all the monks in the area. Here they would assemble to recite the pâtimokkha, or rules of discipline, with a view toward maintaining both personal and collective adherence to the monastic rules of conduct. There were many such rules of conduct, but we will only take a brief look at some of the more important rules that monks and nuns were obliged to follow.

Violation of the following rules would result in permanent expulsion from the sangha: 1) killing a human person, 2) thievery, 3) sexual intercourse, and 4) claiming false spiritual attainment. Monastic life was designed to be an assault on egoism and the passions; one can readily see that these four actions would not be conducive to that end. No human society can condone the killing of one member by another. Unless murder is severely dealt with, the mutual trust and cooperation that defines a community is at risk. Thievery not only promotes avarice but also corrodes trust in one's fellow monks. Monks and nuns were to be celibate and so free to concentrate their energies on their practice rather than on the worldly concerns of marriage, children, and physical appearance. Sexual intercourse was therefore forbidden, although this prohibition is modified in some Mahâyâna sects that allow monks to marry. Even in those cases, the impetus to simplify one's life remains.

The most grievous breach of honesty in monastic life is to claim that you have achieved a goal that all your fellow monks are earnestly striving for when in fact you have not. This egotism strikes at the heart of the Buddhist spiritual community, not least of all because Buddhism espouses a disintegration of egoism as its goal. Other rules in the Vinaya Pitika deal with violations that require a gathering of monastics to deliberate, offences that require a level of punishment short of permanent expulsion, size and site of monastic quarters, required decorum that a monk should show to his senior, and so on.

The applicant for monastic life must meet strict criteria. A person applying for full ordination has to be a minimum of twenty years of age, but one can enter the novitiate (which is a preparatory period for monastic life) any time after the age of eight. Young novices are provided tutors and placed under the guidance of a senior monk who helps to instruct the youngster. To become a monk, a person must be male, of good physical and mental health, unencumbered by military service, free of debt, and carrying his parents' permission. Ordination includes tonsure, which is the shaving of the head. Tonsure signals that the person has left the world. Hair is seen as a sexually attractive feature; it is not needed in the monastery.

The newly ordained monk takes the Three Refuges ("I take refuge in the Buddha, I take refuge in the Dharma, I take refuge in the Sangha.") and vows to abide by the Ten Precepts. The Ten Precepts involve abstention from 1) taking life, 2) stealing, 3) sexual misconduct, 4) lying, 5) drinking alcoholic beverages, 6) eating after noon, 7) watching entertainment, 8) adorning oneself with jewelry or perfumes, 9) using a high bed (here the idea is that a padded bed encourages excess sleep or lounging), and 10) receiving gold or silver. (Buddhist laypersons abide by the first five of these precepts.) The newly ordained monk also receives the robes he will wear as a monk.

The ordination ceremony requires a quorum of at least ten ordained monks. The candidate is presented to the congregation, and it is attested that he has met the minimum requirements. This is followed by a public request for approval by silence. If none of the assembled monks speaks, the person is ordained. The date and time are noted and are important for establishing seniority. If you are ordained five minutes before me, you remain my senior regardless of our relative ages.

The monk then begins his monastic life and duties. You may think that a monk spends his entire day in prayer, meditation, or some other devotional activities. While it is certainly true that monks do engage in prescribed spiritual practice each day, much of the monk's time is filled with routine physical work.

BUDDHIST MONASTICISM: NUNS

According to Buddhist tradition, Gautama Buddha was reluctant to let women into the monastic order but relented due to the entreaty of his disciple, Ânanda. Again, according to tradition, the Buddha stated that if women were indeed allowed to enter monastic life, the dharma would not survive as long as it would with their exclusion. Whether or not the Buddha ever actually made that remark, there appear to have been early Buddhist nuns who were as zealous for the dharma as their male counterparts.

The *Therigâtha*, a collection of songs (gâthas) attributed to elder nuns (theri), sheds light on the women's reasons for entering the monastery. The women came from varied backgrounds. Some were princesses, others housewives, and others courtesans. Some were fleeing poverty, or a difficult marriage, or the boredom of housework. More than half, however, came from a favorable situation and entered the monastery for purely religious reasons: faith in the Buddha's teachings and missionary zeal.

The Buddhist nun's ordination resembles that of a monk, except that she must stand before both a quorum of monks and a quorum of nuns. Nuns must pledge to abide by eight additional regulations that the monks do not follow; these include rules that subordinate the nuns to the monks.

The women's order never received as much financial support as the men's order. Eventually, the Theravâda order of nuns dwindled to almost nothing. There are female monastics in some Mahâyâna sects, but they usually prefer to be called "monks" rather than "nuns," and at least those in the more modern Buddhist sects are not subordinate to male monks.

THE BUDDHIST LAYPERSON

The Buddhist layperson financially supports the temple and patronizes temple events. Laypeople also support the monastic community. It is designed to be a mutually beneficial situation: The patron receives good karma, Buddhist teaching, and spiritual guidance in return for their financial contributions. Lay contributions may be given in the form of alms dispensed to a specific monk during his begging rounds, or as a large annual gift to the temple. Many families do both. Even the small amounts of change given to purchase incense, amulets, or postcards at a temple are part of the economics of the Buddhist temple. The omnipresent expectation that visitors should place coins in a coin box as they pray or receive blessings underscores the mutually assumed dynamic of financial and spiritual exchange. Without the vital and varied support of the lay community, monastic Buddhism could not exist.

The core beliefs of a Buddhist, whether lay or monastic, reside in the Four Noble Truths. The layperson is expected to take the Three Refuges and abide by the Five Precepts. The Five Precepts

FALUN GONG AND LAY BUDDHISM IN CHINA

In the West, many people seem to believe that the People's Republic of China is a Buddhist country. Perhaps they think of it as a country where the kinds of Buddhist beliefs and practices discussed in this book are widely practiced. They may even believe that it has always been predominantly Buddhist and that its people have practiced Buddhism for centuries.

This is not quite an accurate picture. Buddhism was transmitted to China early in the first millennium C.E. It went through historical periods of growth and decline. The current Communist government offers no support for religious belief of any variety, and it certainly considers Buddhism to be a religion. Consequently, lay Buddhist practice in China today is very much on a "folk" level. It would be wrong to leave the reader with the impression that children who grow up Buddhist in China today are extensively schooled in meditation or learn to read Buddhist sutras. In the People's Republic of China today, laypeople who practice Buddhism do so primarily at home altars. They may also go to the temple and pray before the main altar.

There are also new religions that have a Buddhist component. An example of such a new religion is the Falun Gong (also called Falun Dafa) movement. It is one of the more popular religio-philosophical movements in China today. You may have even heard about it on the news, as the Chinese government is very concerned about its rapid growth. What are the basic tenets of Falun Gong, and how do they relate to Buddhism?

Falun Gong is often translated as "Buddhist Law" movement. It was founded by Li Hongzhi (b.1952) who wanted to combine Buddhist and Taoist ideas into a set of morality and meditation practices. It does not call itself a religion as only five religions (Buddhism, Taoism, Islam, Protestantism, and Catholicism) are currently viewed as legal religions by the Chinese government. Anything other than these five religions is deemed illegal and may even be in danger of being labeled a "dangerous cult." That is what happened to Falun Gong.

The primary purpose of Falun Gong is to promote mental and physical health. It is such a popular mass movement (with some forty million followers according to some estimates) that the Chinese government views it as a threat to the well-being of the nation. They have likened Falun Gong to the Aum Shinrikyo movement in Japan. Aum Shinrikyo was responsible for killing people in a Tokyo subway by releasing sarin gas. (There is no reason to believe that Falun Gong ever has or ever would do anything similar.) The Chinese government banned Falun Gong in 1999. Following a very large protest by Falun Gong followers, government suppression of the movement began the following year and continues today.

How many Buddhist elements are found in Falun Gong? The movement teaches karma and rebirth. It utilizes physical exercise as part of a spiritual philosophy that stresses truthfulness, benevolence, and forbearance. Using five key exercises, the practitioner seeks to unleash the power of the Falun (which is viewed as a power centered in the lower abdomen), so it can travel throughout his or her body, thus ensuring physical and spiritual well-being. Falun Gong also teaches that its practices can replace traditional medical treatments for illnesses. The symbol of Falun Gong is a swastika (an ancient Asian symbol often employed by Buddhism) surrounded by yin-yang symbols (the yin-yang circle is a Taoist symbol).

We would have to conclude that Falun Gong's connection with traditional Buddhist teachings is limited. It does, however, use Buddhist and Taoist ideas to attract Chinese people (and an increasing number of people in other countries) to a "new" philosophy.

receive more emphasis in Therâvâda Buddhism than they do in Mahâyâna Buddhism, but all Buddhists are obligated to live an ethical life. As noted previously, all Buddhists believe in rebirth and transmigration and seek nirvana, if not in this life then in a future one.

The main difference between Buddhists is in the practice they choose to employ. The devotional approach, involving praying to a deity, is most common. Other Buddhists rely on meditation, sometimes mixing meditation with prayer.

7

Cultural Expressions

*Children ran to and fro—shrieking and laughing—
stopping only for seconds to stare wide-eyed as a new
performer, clad in wild and colourful costume, made
his entrance. At this too, the expressions of the old men
who sat alone and stony-faced would brighten and for
a moment the old women would cease their chatter.*

—Tenzin Gyatso, His Holiness,
the Fourteenth Dalai Lama,
in *Freedom in Exile*

BUDDHISM AND ART

Buddhism has always been associated with art, probably because Buddhism requires something that art provides, namely, the ability to see things in dramatically unconventional ways. Buddhist paintings and sculpture serve as a focus for meditation for monks and as teachings in pictures for ordinary laypersons. The famed Borobodur Temple in Java (C.E. seventh–eighth century) is one of the world's great sights. It is composed of 13.6 acres of lava, with close to four hundred Buddha statues and nearly six thousand relief scenes.

Visitors to the Hill of Sanchi in the State of Madhya Pradesh, India, can see chronicled on this one site the growth, flourishing, and decay of Buddhist art and architecture in India over a period of around fourteen hundred years. The Buddha images found here and elsewhere follow a carefully prescribed standard of physical proportions, for they are designed to illustrate the physical harmony and beauty of a perfected being, a Buddha. Creating a Buddha image is therefore an exacting science. Perfect proportions are also required in the design of religious monuments like stûpas. Hand positions (mudras) on statues convey an entire spiritual vocabulary—gesturing, teaching, compassion, fearlessness, and much more.

Mandalas, richly decorated and colored geometric designs, are used for meditation. The person meditating is to realize the spiritual power of the mandala within his own being. In Dharamsala, India, Tibetan Buddhist monks spend close to a month painstakingly creating a Kalachakra ("Wheel of Time") mandala from grains of colored sand. After the ceremony is completed, this exquisite mandala is typically destroyed to drive home the truth of impermanence, and the sands are used in an offering for world peace.

Given the fact that Buddhism has produced such a vast array of art, we will not be able to discuss all of it. Let us begin at the beginning, with the earliest known Buddhist art, and proceed from there to a consideration of several representative forms of Buddhist art.

THE BEGINNINGS OF BUDDHIST ART

There is no known surviving Buddhist art until centuries after the time of the Buddha's death. During the Mauryan period (ca. 323–185 B.C.E.), we find the spread of stûpas, stone burial mounds that housed relics of the Buddha. The first recognizably Buddhist buildings and the use of carved caves to serve as temples, shrines, and monastic residences appeared contemporaneously with the spread of the stûpas.

Some of the stûpas have large stone gateways decorated with Buddhist art. The one at Sanchi (near Vidisha in Madhya Pradesh, India) has various Buddhist symbols and events from the Buddha's life carved on it. The foundations for Sanchi date back to the time of Aśoka (273–236 B.C.E.); the carving on several of the gateways can be dated to the first century B.C.E.

Perhaps the earliest Buddhist art is found on Aśoka's pillars. Aśoka inscribed his edicts on wood and stone pillars. These pillars also contained a number of carved images that subsequently served as Buddhist symbols: lotuses, wheels, and lions.

Early Buddhist art did not employ images of the Buddha but did utilize scenes from the *Jataka* stories and other instructional materials. In scenes illustrating the Buddha's prior lives, he is portrayed as an animal (e.g., a deer) rather than as a human being. In scenes from his life as Siddhartha Gautama, he might be represented by an empty throne, the wheel (of the Law), or a stûpa, rather than as a human figure. Portrayals of scenes from these stories were advantageously placed so that pilgrims circumambulating the stûpa would be engaged by them. Although the Buddha was not shown as a human figure, other people were drawn as human beings. Statuary at early sites like Sanchi was an interesting mix of male and female figures, and this influenced the subsequent development of Buddhist statuary.

The first human images of Gautama Buddha appeared in the first century of the Common Era. The first statues differed noticeably depending on whether or not they were influenced by Greek artistic conventions introduced into India at the time of

Alexander the Great. These early images set the pattern for later artistic portrayals of Buddhas and bodhisattvas.

Also in the first century, we see the beginning of painting of Buddhist images, such as in the Ajanta caves in India. Buddhist art flourished in India until about the twelfth century. It also traveled with Buddhism to Sri Lanka, Southeast Asia, East Asia, and Tibet. In each of these areas, Buddhist art blended with local artistic conventions to produce a new and distinctive form of art. While we lack the space to introduce all of these varieties of Buddhist art, we can at least demonstrate the range of Buddhist arts by considering a number of different art forms. In the remainder of this chapter, we will consider the tea ceremony, pagodas, and the *haiku* poetry form. Then we will turn to a brief exploration of Zen art before we conclude this chapter by discussing contemporary Buddhist influences on culture.

A JAPANESE TEA CEREMONY

The way of tea (cha-no-yu), as embodied in the Japanese tea ceremony, is in itself a miniature showcase of Buddhist arts. Architecture, gardening, calligraphy, pottery, and flower arranging, all support the artistry of the tea ceremony itself. Tea and Buddhism have enjoyed a long camaraderie: Tea drinking began in China "among the Zen [Buddhist] monks, who used it as a method of preventing sleep." [70]

Sen no Rikyu, the sixteenth-century Japanese tea master, said, "The art of Cha-no-yu consists of nothing else but boiling water, making tea, and sipping it." His statement underscores the tea ceremony's emphasis on simplicity.

A tea ceremony is a formal event, and one must be invited to attend the event, which is held in a tea garden (chaniwa). The tea garden, along with all the other elements of the tea ceremony, is designed to convey yugen ("mystery"), wabi ("restrained expression"), and sabi ("individual objects"). The tea ceremony and its setting are designed to cultivate a calm mind and demeanor in the participants.

The traditional teahouse is made of natural materials. It has a low door that requires the person entering to bow low in a spirit of humility. The tea room is itself a work of art, and within it are displayed other works of art—maybe an example of ikebana (flower arrangement) or a kakemono (a hanging scroll). Often the tea ceremony utensils are themselves *objet d'art* to be seen and admired. Silence permeates the ceremony; talk is sparingly offered and only in hushed tones. The sounds that surround the participants are those of the natural denizens of the garden, the soft hissing of the teakettle, the slight shuffling on the straw mats, the sipping of the tea.

In his book *Zen and Japanese Culture*,[71] D.T. Suzuki identifies four characteristics of the tea ceremony: harmony (wa), reverence (kei), purity (sei), and tranquility (jaku). Balance or harmony between the elements of the tea ceremony reflects, as Japanese Zen monk Takuan Soho says, "the spirit of a naturally harmonious blending of Heaven and Earth."[72] The tea ceremony cultivates reverence for all natural things and the humility that naturally arises from that reverence. In a physical sense, purity underscores the importance of keeping the tearoom immaculately clean. Symbolically, purity points to the purpose of the ceremony, which is to cleanse the mind and spirit of the accumulated dust of the world. Tranquility permeates the tea ceremony, which is truly a contemplative practice.

The purity and cleanliness of the tea ceremony is artistic, not antiseptic. Not every leaf is raked up in the tea garden; Sen no Rikyu would sweep the path to the tea room and then reach up to a tree limb and shake it to allow new leaves to fall naturally on the path. The tea ceremony endeavors to bring to the participants' awareness the purity that dwells within his or her breast. This is a natural, embodied purity, not the sterility of a disinfected facility.

PAGODAS

Is there any image more characteristic of Asia than the silhouette of a pagoda against the evening sky? The pagoda (which is a Portuguese word) evolved from the design of the stûpa as

Buddhism spread across Asia. In China, it assumed the now-familiar shape of a multitiered tower. There are generally an odd number of tiers, and the number is symbolic: In a five-story pagoda, each story may represent one of the five elements (earth, metal, water, fire, and wood).

Pagodas were constructed in a variety of shapes and materials. As Robert Fisher notes, "A survey of East Asian pagodas reveals a preference for a particular material in each culture, which in turn affected the design. The Chinese preferred the basic shape and brick construction with elaborate surface details that emulate wood. The Koreans favored stone; while the Japanese, with their abundant supply of timber (and relative lack of granite), constructed pagodas of wood."[73]

Like the stûpa, the pagoda is a repository of Buddhist relics. Pagodas had stairways to access the different levels. The Horyûji pagoda, the oldest one in Japan, has four scenes in clay on its first level: 1) on the east side, Vimalakirti and Manjuśri are engaged in a conversation;[74] 2) on the north is represented Gautama Buddha passing into parinirvânâ; 3) on the west, a scene depicts the distribution of Gautama Buddha's relics; and 4) on the south, Maitreya (the future Buddha) is giving a lecture. Paintings on the exterior of the pagoda were also used for instructional purposes.

The pagoda was initially an essential part of Chinese temple design. It stood between the main gate and the main hall, with the assembly hall being placed behind the main hall, thus forming a line of structures. However, in the Sui and Tang periods (581–907), some temples had two pagodas and they were placed on either side of the main hall.

The fact that the pagoda was no longer situated on the main axis of the temple signaled its reduction in importance. The dominant position in the temple now belonged to the main hall. Robert Fisher has called this "a victory for Chinese secularism,"[75] because the design of the main hall was based on the design of an imperial throne hall rather than on the design of any religious structure. The removal of the pagoda from the main axis of the temple, combined with the rise of Pure Land and Ch'an

Buddhism (neither of which placed much importance on relics), ultimately led to a reduced role of the pagoda's presence and usefulness.

HAIKU AND BÂSHO

Sometimes American schoolchildren are introduced to the haiku form of poetry. You might remember being asked to compose a haiku using exactly five syllables in the first line, seven syllables in the second line, and five syllables in the third and final line. Japanese poetry has come to be associated with the haiku, but actually the haiku form is one of a larger assortment of poetic structures, including the tanka (thirty-one syllables in five lines of 5, 7, 5, 7, and 7 syllables respectively) and the sedôka (5–7–7–5–7 syllables).

In China, Korea, and Japan, we find both monastics and laypersons using poetry to express Buddhist ideas. Not just in these countries but in many parts of the world poetry is used to express profound ideas that cannot easily be explained in prose.

The one name most universally associated with haiku is that of Bâsho (C.E. 1644–1694). Born in Ueno, a city near Kyoto, Bâsho followed a rather inauspicious path at the beginning of his life: He became the servant of a relative of the local feudal lord. His master, Todo Yoshitada, enjoyed the exchange of verse (called *haikai*) and Bâsho showed a talent for composing poems. His master's death turned Bâsho's life in a new direction. He journeyed extensively and wrote about his experiences in his many books. He composed poetry constantly. In time, he became quite famous.

He ultimately settled in Edo (present-day Tokyo) where his students had built him a hut. A banana tree was planted in the yard of the hut thus giving rise to his name, Bâsho ("basho" is the Japanese word for banana plant).

Bâsho went on many pilgrimages, and these trips inspired many of his writings, including the collection for which he is best known, *Narrow Road to the Far North*. He also began practicing Zen Buddhism under Priest Butcho (1642–1715).[76]

I have included some examples of Bâsho's poetry below, translated into English. The reader is encouraged to seek out other examples published in books and on the Internet. The poems below do not seem to follow the 5–7–5 syllable structure of haiku, until one remembers that Bâsho was composing in Japanese not English.

> Against the brushwood gate,
> Dead tea leaves swirl
> In the stormy wind.

As you ponder this first poem, recall that the Chinese have for millennia read the configuration of tea leaves in a cup as a means of divining the future.

> The sound of hail
> I am the same as before
> Like that aging oak.

This second poem is a humorous one, reflecting upon the silliness of the author's feeling of security after the storm has passed. He feels secure because nothing has changed, his world has not been uprooted by the storm. That aging oak, for example, doesn't look any different after the storm than it did before, but the very fact that it is "aging" indicates that it has not escaped change. Everything is impermanent.

> Another year is gone.
> A travel hat on my head.
> Straw sandals on my feet.[77]

What does this third poem say to you? It was written at the end of a year of traveling. Although the passage of time is once again indicated, the author seems at ease with this now; indeed, he appears quite content with his life of impermanence. Bâsho died in his fiftieth year but his contributions to world poetry and to the expression of Buddhist ideas endure.

ZEN ART

Shin'ichi Hisamatsu (1889–1980), a noted Zen Master, authored a book translated into English as *Zen and the Fine Arts*.[78] The book includes many examples of what Dr. Hisamatsu identifies as Zen art as well as his rendering of the philosophical basis behind Zen art. He enumerates seven characteristics of the Zen aesthetic: 1) Asymmetry, 2) Simplicity, 3) Austere Sublimity or Lofty Dryness, 4) Naturalness, 5) Subtle Profundity or Deep Reserve, 6) Freedom from Attachment, and 7) Tranquility.

Some of these characteristics echo D.T. Suzuki's comments on the tea ceremony (see page 116). Perhaps by examining each of

BUDDHIST CULTURE VIA *TRICYLE*

One of the more visible signs of the growing popularity of Buddhism in the United States is the appearance of Buddhist-related periodicals. Of these, *Tricycle: The Buddhist Review* is perhaps the best known. ("Tricycle" refers to the three cycles of birth-death-rebirth.) The magazine was first published in the early 1990s and documents what the Editor-in-Chief James Shaheen noted on the occasion of the fiftieth issue: " . . . if you look closely, you'll see that the dharma has found its way into nearly every nook and cranny of our culture, from intensive retreats to often remote locations to the everyday lives of ordinary folks." (7)

Each issue offers a short dharma talk, suggestions on practice, an interview with a famous Buddhist, book reviews, a directory of dharma centers, etc. While the mere existence of this periodical shows that Buddhism has arrived, the articles one encounters on its pages provide even better examples of the spread of the dharma into Western culture.

One finds articles on such topics as contemplation in corporate culture, a Buddhist history of food, and Buddhism in Russia. There is virtually no aspect of Western culture that it has not examined through the lens of Buddhism. That is precisely the point: Western Buddhists and others who are interested in looking at issues and topics in a different way are asking questions like: What does Buddhism have to say about abortion or the war in Iraq? What would Buddhist ethics have to say about such matters as parenting or racial diversity, the environment or gay marriage? Western Buddhists have created an

Hisamatsu's terms we may get a better glimpse not only into Zen art but into the nature of Buddhist art in general. The forms and even the specifics of the underlying philosophy of Buddhist art vary with culture and sect, of course, but the larger intent of Buddhist art, once grasped, will open the door to understanding many different types of Buddhist art.

Asymmetry is closely related to naturalness. Nature is not often symmetrical or perfectly ordered but rather irregular and seemingly, from the human perspective, disordered. Thus, asymmetrical artistic expressions try to capture the way the world truthfully is through a "deformation" of form and perfection.

expectation that there should be an applied Buddhist ethics to accompany their belief and practice.

While writing this, I am perusing the latest issue of *Tricycle* (Spring 2004). I see a special section on Buddhist practice within prisons in the United States. The authors are a diverse group, including current and recently released prisoners as well as those who bring the Buddhist teachings inside the prison walls. The section describes the missionary effort that Buddhism is undertaking in U.S. prisons. As have the other two missionary religions (Christianity and Islam), Buddhism is reaching out to an imprisoned audience. One article speaks of Scott Darnell who is serving a life sentence for first-degree murder in a prison in Illinois. Darnell writes:

> I count myself fortunate to have learned the Buddha-way during my time inside. I count myself blessed beyond measure to have known people who strive for truth, understanding, and transformation, both for themselves and others. If such a thing is possible here, surely it is possible everywhere. Buddha-nature shines forth right here, right now, for anyone willing to look. Do any of us here see completely? No. But at the end of our sangha gatherings each week, somehow things appear different. If but for a moment, the gun towers seem not as tall, the razor wire not as sharp. Instead, there is blue sky, the warmth of the sun on our faces, and world engaged and engaging. (77)

Simplicity is present in the Japanese teahouse, the brushwork of the calligrapher, and the core of the Buddhist belief system. Of course, mandalas can be quite ornate, and certain Buddhist rituals are elaborate, but even the most ornate examples of Buddhist art retain a kind of simplicity because they put the viewer in touch with childlike abandon and the freedom of emptiness. As Hisamatsu explains:

> Simplicity also has something in common with naïveté and abandon. For, actually, it is abandon rather than deliberateness that is in keeping with Simplicity. The ultimate Simplicity is "not a single thing," or the One. If, as the negation of holiness results in the freedom of non-holiness, then simplicity as the negation of clutter may be spoken of as being "boundless"—there is nothing limiting, as in a cloudless sky.[79]

Perhaps another way to approach the sometimes complex simplicity of Zen art is to think of it as a simplicity on the far side of complexity rather than a simple simplicity.

Austere Sublimity focuses our attention on the deeper, mature aspect of nature. It is a "becoming dried," with the "disappearance of childishness, unskillfulness or inexperience, with only the pith or essence remaining."[80]

Naturalness means not artificial in a general sense; however, it has an additional meaning for Buddhists who believe that our original nature is the Buddha nature. A genuine work of Buddhist art is one that expresses Awakening in one way or another.

Subtle Profundity implies that Buddhist art should convey a deeper level beneath the surface impression, a level that is indicative of the artist's spiritual state. An excellent example of this is the dry-landscape garden at Ryôanji in Kyoto, Japan. Ryôanji is a Rinzai Zen temple founded in 1450. It is renowned throughout the world for its exemplary rock garden. Consisting of fifteen larger rocks and smaller rocks that are raked, the garden appears rather stark and unassuming. The garden is actually a meditation tool, not unlike the mandala. The monks will meditate in its presence with the intent of realizing the nondifference between the garden and themselves. The garden is, in essence, a koan.

The Zen rock garden may evoke some element of subtle profundity in the casual observer, or it may not. The profundity it exhibits is the reflection of the Awakened mind of its creator and the mirroring of that reflection in the mind of the observer. In Buddhist belief, there is nonduality, no distinction, between the two minds. Hisamatsu refers to this "reflection" as "an infinite echo reverberating from a single thing." This single thing, as we now know from our study of Buddhism, "contains everything." [81]

Hisamatsu associates this characteristic of Zen art with a "calm darkness" such as one would encounter in the tearoom. Such darkness may be understood as "calming darkness," which can bring tranquility and relief to the participant. He also refers to this as a "bright darkness." [82]

Freedom from Attachment is a cardinal Buddhist idea as embodied in the Four Noble Truths—each person is to be released (Awakened) from his or her egoistic passions. Here the emphasis is on the transcendence of the conventions, authority, and rules that attend dualistic thinking. What is meant is not a willful arbitrariness borne from embracing chaos but a by-product of Awakened consciousness that allows the artist to be naturally unrestrained in word or action. For example, in the môndo (Zen dialogue) all conventions of grammar or meaning are seemingly suspended, as can be seen in the following example:

> When Yüeh shan (Jp.: Yakusan) was sitting in meditation, a monk asked, "What are you thinking while sitting immovably?"
>
> The master said, "I am thinking of the very matter of not-thinking."
>
> To this the monk asked, "How do you think of the matter of not-thinking?"
>
> The master replied, "*Non*-thinking!" [83]

Again, this is not meant to be nonsensical or mere wordplay but a display of the interlocutor's spiritual state. Hisamatsu notes that the Zen tradition calls this the "Rule of No Rule." [84]

The "Rule of No Rule" applies not only in words but also in other art forms.

Tranquility is the seventh characteristic. Zen art and, by extension, Buddhist art is meant to convey a tranquility, a composure within the participant. Even in the most elaborate display of color, complexity, or noise, Buddhist art maintains its peace-producing core.

BUDDHIST CONTRIBUTIONS TO CONTEMPORARY WESTERN ART AND CULTURE

Many Westerners may associate Buddhist art with the Buddhist statue of Maitreya in his Hotei incarnation. This was once a very popular curio. It portrayed a rotund, seated Buddha—one could even rub his belly for good luck!

The West has also displayed an interest in more serious Buddhist art. Most major museums have at least some representative Buddhist pieces, and there are some amazing personal collections of Asian Art, including Buddhist art. Buddhist art has not generally been found in the homes of average Westerners, but this is changing as more Westerners have access to information about Buddhism.

Another important factor in the increasing acceptance of Buddhist art has been the personality of the Dalai Lama and the corresponding growing popularity of Tibetan Buddhist art. One is no longer surprised to see religious items such as prayer flags, framed mandalas, or thangkas in people's homes or displayed on the pages of popular magazines. One may wonder if these objects maintain their sacred nature in the homes of non-Buddhists, where they are most often displayed for their unique design and use of color. Chinese and Japanese Buddhist art has been displayed in Western homes for centuries without any religious connotations. To date, the Asian visual arts have had the most influence in the West; the performing arts (such as dance, music, and theater) have garnered only a limited audience.

Non-Asian converts to Buddhism provide another avenue by which Buddhist art has influenced the West. Henry David

Thoreau (1817–1862), famed naturalist and author of *Walden*, was very interested in Buddhism. Thoreau learned about Eastern texts from his friend, Ralph Waldo Emerson. Western philosophers—including Arthur Schopenhauer, Martin Heidegger, Jean Paul Sartre, and others—have become interested in Buddhism. Western writers and poets connected with the "Beat generation" (Gary Snyder, Alan Ginsberg, and Jack Kerouac, among others) were or are influenced by Buddhism. Western interest in Zen Buddhism has remained strong over the last fifty or so years. More recently, Tibetan Buddhism has attracted the attention of many in the West. Several noted celebrities have publicly embraced Tibetan Buddhism. In a culture that closely follows celebrities' lives, such personal decisions can lead to a broader acceptance of the religion in question. In centuries past, it was critical to convert the king to Buddhism for Buddhism to become established in a new country. Perhaps in the twenty-first century, the new "kings" who need to be converted so that the general populace will follow are the people seen on television and in the movies!

Currently, the most outspoken and famous celebrity proponent of Buddhism is actor Richard Gere. He has starred in many movies over a long career and won an Academy Award for Best Actor in *An Officer and a Gentleman*. Gere has devoted much time and money to the Tibetan Buddhist cause and considers the Dalai Lama to be his teacher.

Recent movies with Buddhist themes include *Kundun*, *Little Buddha*, and the *Matrix* series. Buddhists in the music world include John Cage, Laurie Anderson, Tina Turner, and members of the rock group The Beastie Boys. The "New Age" movement has encouraged and supported many Buddhist musical presentations, both live and recorded. The West has also been treated to the considerable musical talents of Tibetan monks on tour. The monks use traditional instruments to accompany the chanting of sutras.

Still, no form of Buddhism seems as cemented to the American psyche as Zen Buddhism. The interest in Zen manifests in Zen garden design, two-dimensional and three-dimensional art forms, poetry, and even Zen comics! Ironically, today the leading edge of Buddhist art may well be in the West.

8

Holidays

Throughout the centuries
preceding Tibet's invasion by China,
the seasons were marked by numerous festival days . . .
celebrated by monks and laymen alike.
For the latter, the time was passed in eating,
drinking, singing, dancing and playing games,
combined intermittently with prayer.

—Tenzin Gyatso, His Holiness,
the Fourteenth Dalai Lama,
in *Freedom in Exile*

U sually Buddhists have sought to permeate cultures rather than to dominate them. Buddhism, like most other religions, is certain that it knows the truth, but its concept of truth is inclusive rather than exclusive and allows for varying degrees of understanding of truth. This means that Buddhism has often been willing to cooperate with non-Buddhist cultural elements, rather than competing with them. As you will observe in this chapter, this element of cooperation is evident even in Buddhist holidays, many of which have secular elements or elements derived from other religions.

In some countries, Buddhist holidays are determined based upon a lunar calendar; in others, the Western or Gregorian calendar, which is a solar calendar, is used. This means that the dates of certain holidays may vary from country to country. Considering that Buddhists live in many different countries, one would expect some variation in the dates of holidays even without this complication.

There is no universal Buddhist calendar; the many different schools or sects of Buddhism maintain separate calendars. While almost every day of the year is a special observance for Buddhists somewhere, there are major holidays that most Buddhists observe. We begin this chapter with a discussion of several of these more universally observed holidays.

NEW YEAR

Every country in the world celebrates the New Year, and Buddhist countries are no exception. Many countries observe the New Year with a mixture of secular and religious rituals and Buddhist countries do too.

The year 2000 on the Gregorian calendar roughly coincided with the year 2543 B.E. (Buddhist Era). The date of the Buddhist New Year varies from country to country and according to the type of Buddhism practiced. Chinese, Koreans, and Vietnamese celebrate in late January or early February according to the lunar calendar, while the Tibetans usually celebrate about one month later. All of these are Mahâyâna Buddhist nations.

In Theravâda nations (Thailand, Myanmar, Sri Lanka, Cambodia, and Laos) the New Year festival occurs in mid-April. The exact date depends upon the first full moon in April. In Thailand, the date is fixed on April 13.

In general, Asians view the New Year as the most significant cultural celebration of the year. In Asian communities, New Year is equated with family reunions, completing business transactions, ending feuds, making amends, refurbishing wardrobes, honoring ancestors, and cleaning house.

Songkran

The Thai New Year is called *Songkran*. Buddhist images in homes and in the temple are cleansed with jasmine-scented water on the first official day of the New Year. Throughout the world, the New Year is commonly associated with some sort of cleaning ritual.

In addition to cleansing, water is also used for veneration. As a sign of respect, young people will sprinkle water on older people.

The family will dress in traditional Thai clothing and wear leis of jasmine. Faces and necks will be painted with a white paste to ward off evil. To signify the connectedness of all people, people will tie strings to each other's wrists accompanied by prayers of blessing. The strings are to be worn until they fall off on their own.

Chinese New Year

New Year's is an auspicious day in China as well, where it is actually a season rather than a day. (This is analogous to the Christmas season, which surrounds Christmas Day.) The Chinese family will use the occasion for cleaning, including applying new paint, often red (the color of life), to the house. Other decorations are put up signifying best wishes and special food is placed on the family altar. The eve of the New Year finds family members gathered for a common meal with special foods being served. Also on this evening, places of worship will be visited for special New Year blessings. On New Year's Day itself, children may receive presents from their parents, neighbors are visited, and a fresh start is brought to relationships that may be strained or inactive. The famed Lantern Festival occurs at the end of the New Year season (on the fifteenth day of the year). People carry lanterns into the streets to take part in a great parade. One version of the origin of this festival is Buddhist.

BUDDHA DAY (VESAK)

The most important observance for Buddhists is the commemoration of the birth, Awakening, and death (parinirvâṇâ) of the Buddha. Although it is not believed that all three events actually happened on the same date, Theravâda Buddhists celebrate them all on the same day. This day, sometimes called "Buddha Day" in the West, is known as Vesak or Visakah Puja in Theravâda countries. Traditionally, this day is celebrated on the first full moon day in May (in a leap year it is held in June). On this day, laypeople will go to the temples, participate in a worship service, listen to talks on the dharma, bring food to donate to the temple, and perhaps reaffirm their allegiance to the Five Precepts. It is a joyous occasion and there may be booths on the temple grounds that sell sweets, Buddhist curios, and the like.

In Mahâyâna countries, three separate holidays commemorate the Buddha's birth (eighth day of the fourth month), Awakening (eighth day of the twelfth month), and death (fifteenth day of the second month). Buddhists who use the Western calendar (such as Japanese and American Buddhists) do not celebrate these holidays on the exact same day as Buddhists who follow the lunar calendar.

DHARMA DAY (ASALHA PUJA DAY)

Dharma Day is primarily a Theravâda holiday, although it should be noted that there is a Tibetan equivalent that occurs about a month earlier. Dharma Day is observed in Thailand and some other countries in Southeast Asia.

Dharma Day is also called Asalha Puja Day, because it falls on the first full-moon day of the eighth lunar month, and the eighth

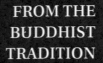

FROM THE
BUDDHIST
TRADITION

A painting of the Birth of the Buddha, Temple of Yongju, Suwon, South Korea. The Buddha, or Siddhartha Gautama, was born in Lumbinî, in what is now Nepal, in 563 B.C.E. It is said that Siddhartha miraculously emerged from his mother's side and thus did not experience the trauma of a typical birth. He therefore was able to remember all of his previous lives due to this Awakening experience.

Housed in the School of Ratanakosin, Thonburi District, Thailand, this mural displays the miraculous nature of the Buddha as he raises himself up in front of his family.

This Pancharaksha manuscript, housed at the Newark Museum, Newark, New Jersey, dates to the twelfth century C.E. These two folios are written in Sanskrit on palm leafs.

This eighteenth-century gilded bronze prayer wheel contains a long prayer scroll and is housed at the Musee des Arts Asiatiques-Guimet, Paris, France. Known as *chhos-hkor* in Tibetan, prayer wheels are often carried by pilgrims on visits to temples. When the wheel is spun, it is said to bring spiritual blessings and well-being to the world.

The shrine to the Golden Buddha at Deskit Monastery in Nubra Valley, India.

The Buddha of Bamiyan. This two-hundred-foot statue located in central Afghanistan dates to the fifth century C.E. Though it was one of two statues of the Buddha destroyed by the Taliban in 2001, there are plans to have it rebuilt.

After achieving enlightenment, Gautama Buddha traveled to Sarnath—located in present-day Uttar Pradesh, India—where he preached the first discourse on the Four Noble Truths. Indian Emperor Ashoka is said to have erected these stupas on the site where the Buddha preached his famous sermon.

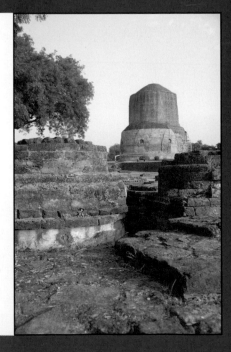

Tibetans believe that prayer flags carry their prayers and mantras to heaven as offerings to their deities, and benefit those who hang them, as well as all sentient beings. These flags have been strung near Potala Palace, Lhasa, Tibet, the original home of Tenzin Gyatso, the fourteenth Dalai Lama.

A replica of Byodoin Temple, Kyota, Japan. The original temple, which was built in the twelfth century, still stands today and is one of the few temples that remain from Japan's Heian period. This reproduction is located on the island of Oahu, Hawaii.

month on the Buddhist calendar is named *Asalha*. Dharma Day celebrates the Buddha's first teaching.

The Buddha attained Awakening on the full moon of the sixth lunar month. Two months later, on the full moon of the eighth lunar month, he delivered his first sermon to his first five disciples in Deer Park. This event marked the establishment of the Buddhist religion.

There are a variety of activities that might take place on Dharma Day, but one common activity is the chanting of the discourse known as the Dhamma Cakka Sutta ("the Setting in Motion of the Wheel of Truth"). The chanting would ordinarily take place in the original Pali language and form part of the evening vigil.

Other activities might include a visit to a monastery, listening to a sermon, joining a procession, or attending an award ceremony in which scholarships are presented to schoolchildren from low-income families. The scholarships are funded by the monastery.

SANGHA DAY (MAGHA PUJA DAY)

You may have noted a Buddha Day and a Dharma Day, and you might recall that the "Three Jewels" of Buddhism are the Buddha, the Dharma, and the Sangha. Logically, you might expect a Sangha Day, and you would be correct. Occurring on the first full moon of the third lunar month, Buddhists recall on this day a significant event in the life of the Buddha.

After the initial Rains Retreat (Vassa), the Buddha traveled to Rajagraha where he met up with 1,250 arhats who had, without prior appointment, convened to pay homage to the Buddha. This day is also called "Fourfold Assembly Day" because there are four important elements: The number of arhats who convened, the fact that all had been ordained by the Buddha himself, the fact that all came without appointment, and the fact that all this occurred on a full-moon day.

Having looked at some of the more universally observed Buddhist holidays, we turn now to some examples of holidays that are associated with a given area. We begin with two East Asian festivals (Obon and the Hungry Ghost Festival). After discussing the Festival of the Tooth in Sri Lanka, we move on to two Vajrayâna festivals (the Tibetan feast of Tara and Padmasambhava Day in Bhutan). We will conclude this chapter with a look at a special Japanese Buddhist ritual known as the Sennichi Kaihôgyô.

OBON [85]

Ancestor worship is common in East Asia. It is not surprising, then, that Ulambana or Ancestors' Day is more popular in

BUDDHIST ENVIRONMENTAL PRACTICE: THE ORDINATION OF TREES

Many people have noted Buddhism's earth-friendly attitude. There is even an emerging body of scholarship on what might be called a Buddhist environmental ethic. Here I would like to discuss an interesting response to deforestation on the part of some Thai Buddhist monks. The response involves the appropriation of a traditional ritual (monastic ordination) in a creative response to an emerging need (saving the trees).

Phrakhru Manas Natheepitak, the abbot of the Wat Bodharma in northern Thailand, is credited with devising "tree ordination" [86] in the early 1990s as a response to the continued deforestation near his temple ("wat" means temple). He thought that if the trees became sacred by being "ordained" (just as a monk or a nun does), no one would dare to cut them down. He hoped that his "tree ordinations" would also help publicize the environmental devastation the entire country of Thailand was experiencing due to deforestation.

Phrakhru Manas had tried every avenue he knew to get the logging company to stop cutting down trees but to no avail. Despite concerns from Buddhists and his own temple, he persisted and this practice has now spread across Thailand.

In July 1991, in the Nan Province, Phrakhru Pitak Nanthakhun conducted a tree ordination. [87] Typically, the laity provides donations

East Asian countries than anywhere else. Ulambana is primarily observed in Mahâyâna traditions, but some in the Theravâda tradition observe this holiday as well. In Japan, Ulambana is known as Obon, and in China it is the Hungry Ghost Festival.

Obon is observed in summer, traditionally in July but recently this festival has been moved to August. School is out and many people take this time to travel to their ancestral homes where they can return to their roots. Obon thus becomes a massive family reunion of the living and, as will shortly become apparent, of the dead.

to the monks prior to an ordination ceremony. In this case, nurseries and patrons had donated twelve hundred seedlings to the monks. During the ceremony, several plays not only provided entertainment but also highlighted the environmental import of the day.

After sanctifying the robes and seedlings, the officiating monks, led by Phrakhru Pitak, planted some of the seedlings on the temple grounds, next to the tree that was to be ordained, and gave the balance to the attending laity. As the trees had been deemed holy, laypersons would not intentionally harm them for fear of negative karma.

About two hundred people along with twenty monks then traveled to the site of the tree ordination. The tree, one of the oldest still standing in this area, had been prepared and at the appropriate moment was wrapped with the orange robes that would have been wrapped around a human who was being ordained. In Thai human ordinations, the acolyte's begging bowl contains sanctified water that is sprinkled on the participants. However, at this unique gathering, Phrakhru Pitak had ten headmen from local villages drink the water as a sign of their oath to protect the forest.

A plaque attached to the ordained tree reads, *"Tham laay paa khee tham laay chaat,"* which can be translated in several ways due to multiple meanings for the word *chaat*: "To destroy the forest is to destroy life (or "one's rebirth," or "the nation")."

This new use of an ancient ritual demonstrates Buddhism's ability to adapt to emerging social needs. "Tree ordination" appears consistent with the Buddhist sanction to uproot suffering.

As Obon approaches, fires burn at entrances to village homes, and paper lanterns hang in cemeteries. Buddhist family altars are covered with vegetables and fruits are set out as offerings. It is said that soon the ancestors, the spirits of the dead, will be returning to their earthly homes for a visit with their relatives.

Family crests are displayed and mukae-bi (welcoming fires) are lighted to guide the spirits of the dead back home. There they will be greeted by the living members of their family, many of whom will have traveled great distances to return to the site of their family tomb (ohaka). (Most Japanese people now live and work in big cities, but the ohaka, reflecting the demographics of a former era, tend to be in the small towns and in the countryside.)

For several days, the spirits of the dead will be entertained by fireworks and folk dances. The living will pray for the repose of the souls of their ancestors. Buddhist temples will conduct special ceremonies and graveyards will be full of activity as families visit family tombs.

At the conclusion of the holiday, the ancestral spirits will be guided back to the other world by miniature boats carrying lighted candles. The tiny boats are set afloat on a river or in the sea.

HUNGRY GHOST FESTIVAL[88]

In Taiwan and in Chinese communities around the world, the Hungry Ghost Festival occurs at the midpoint of the seventh lunar month (generally in August on the Western calendar). In Taiwan, people refer to the seventh lunar month as "Ghost Month," because during this month those suffering in hell are given a reprieve. The gates of hell are flung open on the first day of the month, allowing the suffering and starving ghosts to roam the earth. They will enjoy a month of feasting and fun before returning to hell on the last day of the month.

The Hungry Ghost Festival combines Confucian, Buddhist, and Taoist elements. The Confucian tradition expects children to show great reverence for their parents, a virtue known as "filial piety." This includes veneration of one's ancestors. The soul that is neglected by its descendants will be hungry and spiteful, and will likely cause trouble for the living. It becomes a "hungry ghost." However, if nonrelatives feed the hungry ghosts during Ghost Month, they will be appeased and not bother the community.

Buddhists celebrate the Hungry Ghost Festival as an expression of compassion, a key Buddhist virtue. They tell the story of Mu-lien's mother, a very selfish woman who was confined to the depths of hell. Mu-lien brought food to the monks on his mother's behalf, and his mother was released from her suffering. Buddhists call the Festival "Ulambana," from a Sanskrit word meaning "the emptying out of hell."

The Taoists call the Hungry Ghost Festival "Putu," signifying a general amnesty for the souls in hell. They also call it "Zhong Yuan." On this day, the Ruler of Earth (Zhong) is said to pardon the sins of human beings.

Who are the ghosts? Not all of them are great sinners. A ghost is anyone who was not lucky enough to become an ancestor. Since burial represents the first stage in sending an ancestor to his or her proper place in the afterlife, anyone who receives an improper burial, or none at all, cannot become an ancestor. The spirit is left homeless. This typically occurs in mass executions, forced migrations, and so forth. Other souls become ghosts because their anger will not let them go to their rest. Perhaps they were murdered, or unjustly executed, and are seeking vengeance.

It is one's descendants who carry out the sacrifices that transform a deceased person into an ancestor. Thus a child who dies, or a woman who is unmarried or barren, becomes a ghost. A person who becomes a Christian, and no longer venerates the ancestors, risks demoting his or her parents to the status of a ghost.

The ghosts are guided by "salvation lanterns" placed at the front door of people's homes, or at the entrances and exits of villages. The lanterns are lit at midnight after burning incense and paying tribute to the lost souls, and extinguished the next morning. They are lit every night of Ghost Month.

At the festival, the ghosts find all kinds of foods prepared for them. Joss paper money will be burned, so they can take it back with them to provide for their needs in the underworld. They are entertained with dances, opera, parades and floats, singing, puppet shows, acrobatics, poetry and painting, and theater troupes.

The festivities come to an end when a Taoist monk dressed up as Zhong Kui begins his dance. Zhong Kui is the Chinese ghost buster. He performs a Taoist dance designed to chase off ghosts who are hesitant to go back to the world of darkness. As the dance ends, the gates of hell are closed for another year.

THE FESTIVAL OF THE TOOTH

The Festival of the tooth is the most important of Sri Lanka's public holidays. It is purely coincidental that it takes place in Kandy, a city in central Sri Lanka. The tooth in question is reputedly a relic of the Buddha. According to the traditional story, a monk plucked one of the Buddha's teeth from the pile of ashes left after his cremation. The tooth was given to Sri Lanka for safekeeping around C.E. 300.

This tooth is housed in a great temple on a small hill. The temple was built specifically to house the tooth, which is kept hidden inside a nested set of caskets and is never seen. However, once a year, in July or August, on a full-moon night, there is a procession held in its honor.

The procession travels through the city of Kandy for ten consecutive nights, growing in size with each night. It includes torchbearers, whip-crackers, dancers, drummers, and many elephants. The casket containing the tooth is carried on the last elephant. The procession begins and ends at the temple on the hill, which is one of the most revered Buddhist temples in the world.

FEAST OF TARA[89]

Tara is a Tibetan Buddhist bodhisattva and the national goddess of Tibet. (Bodhisattvas are treated as deities in Tibet.)

Her feast day falls in summer, in late July or early August on the Western calendar.

Tara is called the "Mother of All Buddhas" because buddhas are born of the wisdom that she represents. She is believed to be able to eliminate the eight fears that, according to Vajrayâna Buddhism, cloud our judgment and keep us from seeing the light of truth. Buddhists believe that the mind is the source of much suffering. Once purified, however, it reflects reality like a pond of still, clear water reflects images—without distortion.

There are two stories regarding Tara's origins. One begins with another bodhisattva who had been working for a long time to guide beings toward Awakening. He had helped hundreds of thousands, but when he realized how many more were still suffering in the cycle of births and deaths, he began to cry. Tara sprang forth from his tears of compassion, saying, "Don't worry—I will help you."

The other story tells about one of Tara's previous births as a human being. She was praying as two monks passed her on the road. One monk said to the other that she showed so much devotion that she would probably be reborn as a man. (The belief at the time was that only men could attain Awakening.) Tara overheard the remark and replied that there is no essential difference between male and female. She then vowed to work perpetually for the benefit of all beings in the body of a woman, no matter how many times she was reborn.

Tara was one of the first female deities in Buddhism. Today, male and female deities are paired in Tibetan Buddhism, just as they are in Hinduism. However, the symbolism of male and female is reversed in the two religions. In Hinduism, the female deity is the active partner (compassion), while the male is more contemplative (wisdom). In Tibetan Buddhism, it is the female partner who is quiescent wisdom itself, while male deities symbolize active compassion. Tara is portrayed with green skin, clothed in silken garments and jeweled ornaments. Her right hand gestures supreme generosity, while her left hand near her heart indicates the bestowing of refuge. She is seated in an unusual lotus position: Her left leg is withdrawn to symbolize renunciation of the world, but her right leg is extended to show that she is always ready to rise to the aid of anyone who needs help.

PADMASAMBHAVA HONORED
IN BHUTAN'S FESTIVALS [90]

The Kingdom of Bhutan lies in the heart of the Himalaya Mountains. Along with Tibet and Mongolia, it comprises the traditional stronghold of Vajrayâna Buddhism, also known as "Tibetan Buddhism." With Mongolia and Tibet currently under Chinese rule, Bhutan is the only surviving nation in the world to have Vajrayâna Buddhism as its official religion.

Padmasambhava ("lotus-born"), a wonder-working teacher who hailed from northern India, introduced Vajrayâna Buddhism to the entire Himalayan region. Many of Bhutan's festivals include dramatized scenes from his life.

Legend says that Padmasambhava made the trip to Bhutan on the back of a flying tigress. The pilgrimage centers of Bhutan tell the story of his visit. At Taktsang, he is said to have conquered the demon spirits that were standing in the way of the spread of Buddhism. In Bumthang, a temple was built on the spot where Padmasambhava's fingerprints and footprints appeared etched into solid rock. Throughout Bhutan, stûpas line the roadsides commemorating places where Padmasambhava stopped to meditate. The people of Bhutan live where Padmasambhava walked. To them, he is the "second Buddha."

THE SENNICHI KAIHÔGYÔ [91]

Sennichi Kaihôgyô is not a festival *per se* but rather a special ceremony. This fascinating one-thousand-day ritual involves arduous mountain hikes. So difficult is it that it has seldom been attempted: less than fifty monks have tried it since 1571.

The ritual is conducted on Mount Hiei, which is a sacred mountain just outside Kyoto. Mount Hiei is the headquarters of the Tendai sect. Any monk who is interested in attempting this ritual must be single, ordained, and must have lived in the Mount Hiei area for twelve years of training. He must also receive permission from the Tendai leadership.

A monk who embarks on the ritual is clad in white (the Buddhist color of death). He wears a symbolic dagger and carries a length of rope. These symbols associated with death signify that death is preferable to quitting, and they also indicate that the pilgrim is not in the world during this ritual period. On his feet, the monk wears straw sandals or just tabi (thin socks) after the first three hundred days.

The monk walks a route over the face of Mount Hiei for one hundred days in a row. There are two routes: one that is twenty-two miles and one that is twenty-five miles. The monk, who starts walking about midnight, will stop to pray and chant a mantra at numerous sites. As it takes about six or seven hours to complete the trek, once accustomed to it, the monk returns to his temple early in the morning and is then expected to keep his regular daytime schedule of duties and activities. On one of the one hundred days, the monk will complete a thirty-mile walk throughout Kyoto with the purpose of transferring the merit he has accumulated to others.

In the Sennichi Kaihôgyô, one such one hundred-day period is completed every spring for three years in a row. This is followed by a fourth and a fifth year, in which the ritual extends to two hundred days. After finishing the accumulated total of seven hundred days of walking, the monk faces an especially difficult interlude.

Called the dôiri (Jp.: "to enter the hall"), the interlude consists of a nine-day period during which the monk does not eat, drink, or sleep. During the dôiri, the monk is restricted to a temple and maintains a seated lotus position in front of a statute of Fudô (a Buddha), and he conducts Buddhist services from that position. Each day at two in the morning, he leaves the temple to walk to a well 656 feet away where he draws water to offer to Fudô. The monk has several attendants who remain with him at all times to keep him from falling asleep. These attendants accompany him to the well, chanting prayers and verses from a sutra. They are not allowed to aid or assist him in any way. As the nine days go by, the relatively short trip to the well takes longer and longer for the monk to complete. However, the monk also attracts more onlookers as the days go by who urge him along with their own prayers and chants.

After the successful completion of the dôiri, the following spring finds the monk completing another one-hundred-day period but now with a thirty-seven mile hike that takes fifteen hours each day to complete. For the seventh and last year of the Sennichi Kaihôgyô, the monk undertakes a fifty-two mile walk through Kyoto called the ômawari. The ômawari involves frequent devotions and again allows him to share his accumulated merit with others. This route requires eighteen hours to complete, so the monk gets very little sleep for this one-hundred-day period. On the last one-hundred-day period, the monk returns to the short route and the ritual is completed.

Memories

This is the way: try, try, try!
Then, over time, there is hope.

—Tenzin Gyatso, His Holiness,
the Fourteenth Dalai Lama,
in *The World of Tibetan Buddhism*

Buddhists have never cherished the memory of historical events as much as they have cherished the spiritual insights of certain teachers. Following this Buddhist orientation, this chapter will profile a few of the more significant personages in Buddhist history. The integral role of the Buddha is self-evident, but we have already discussed his life and teachings. There are others, however, who bear closer study. From the potentially very long list of important Buddhist teachers, I have selected five to serve as illustrations of some of the amazing personalities within Buddhism. We will read of Buddhist practitioners from Japan, Tibet, India, China, and the United States.

Dôgen [92] (1200–1253)

Dôgen was mentioned when discussing Zen Buddhism in Japan and the development of the Sôto sect was attributed to his work. Dôgen was born in Kyoto in 1200 to an aristocratic family. His father was a high-ranking minister in the Japanese government.

Dôgen was considered a precocious child with a quick intellect that allowed him, so the story goes, to read Chinese poetry at four years of age and a Chinese Buddhist treatise at nine.[93] However, his father died when Dôgen was two years old, and his mother's death when he was seven rendered him an orphan. It may be that these events awakened in him a sense of his own finitude that precipitated the events of his adult life.

At thirteen, Dôgen became a monk in the Tendai sect on Mount Hiei right outside Kyoto. After about a year of study, Dôgen started having problems with his practice. In his own words, his overriding question was, "If all beings possess buddha nature, then why is it that one must strive after realizing such in Awakening?"[94] A theist might frame Dôgen's question in this way: "If God is all-loving, all-forgiving, and will act for my salvation, why is it necessary for me to work out my own salvation?"[95]

Dôgen asked his teacher for an answer to his question, but he was not satisfied with the answer he received. He decided to leave Mount Hiei and look for another teacher. (It is interesting to note that when Siddhartha Gautama had questions that could not be answered to his satisfaction by those around him, he too went searching for someone who could provide a better answer.)

Dôgen was referred to Eisai, the Buddhist master responsible for establishing the Rinzai Zen sect in Japan, and he traveled to Kennin-ji. Eisai met Dôgen and responded to his question by saying, "All the Buddhas in the three stages of time are unaware that they are endowed with the Buddha nature, but cats and oxen are well aware of it indeed." [96] This answer satisfied Dôgen and he decided to stay and practice with Eisai. However, Eisai died the following year.

One of Eisai's students, Myôzen (1184–1225), succeeded Eisai at Kennin-ji and Dôgen studied with him for the next nine years. At twenty-three, Dôgen decided to travel to China in order to study Zen and Myôzen accompanied him.

Once in China, Dôgen went to study at T'ien-t'ung monastery with the Abbot Wu-chi. His practice advanced but, still not satisfied, he decided to travel around China looking for the right teacher. Meanwhile, Wu-chi died and his successor, Ju-ching (1163–1228), had a reputation as an excellent teacher. Dôgen returned to T'ien-t'ung for a last attempt to find the right teacher before returning to Japan.

This was a fortunate decision as Ju-ching turned out to be the perfect teacher for him. Ju-ching worked tirelessly at his zazen, inspiring Dôgen to intensify his practice. Finally, Dôgen experienced Awakening:

> Early one morning, as he was making his usual round of inspection at the beginning of the formal zazen period, Ju-ching discovered one of the monks dozing. Scolding the monk, he said, "The practice of zazen is dropping away of body and mind. What do you expect to accomplish by dozing?" Upon hearing these words, Dôgen suddenly realized enlightenment, his Mind's eye opening fully. [97]

His Awakening was accepted by Ju-ching and after continuing his training at the monastery for two more years, Dôgen returned to Japan in 1227. Ju-ching supported his student's decision, hoping that Dôgen would be able to teach the dharma in meaningful ways to the Japanese.

Dôgen initially returned to Kennin-ji and remained there for three years. However, he was never one to stay in one place for very long. He soon moved to another temple, An'yô-in. He had also begun to write by this point. He then moved to Kôshô-ji and began in earnest to train others in his understanding of Zen. It was during this period of time that he wrote what came to be considered his magnum opus, the *Shôbôgenzô Zuimonki*. As his fame as a teacher increased, so too did the demands on his time and the jealousies of other Buddhist groups.

He eventually moved to the temple with which he is most closely associated, Eiheiji—now one of the head temples of the Sôtô sect of Zen Buddhism.

Dôgen had some interest in influencing political events and he met with various leaders. However, his priority was always on persuading others to pursue the practice of Zen through his teaching and writings.

In 1252, Dôgen became ill and returned to Kyoto to seek medical treatment. He died on August 28, 1253, at Seido-in in Takatsuji, Kyoto.

Tenzin Gyatso: The Fourteenth Dalai Lama (1935–)

Undoubtedly the most famous Buddhist monk alive is the Dalai Lama. "Dalai Lama" is not a name but a title. It comes from the Mongolian language, in which "Dalai" means "ocean" and "Lama" means "teacher." The ocean is a symbol of large and deep wisdom. The title was attached to the position in the sixteenth century, when the Mongols ruled the country we now call Tibet.

Traditionally, the Dalai Lama has been the political and spiritual leader of Tibet. The current Dalai Lama's name is Tenzin Gyatso. How does one become a Dalai Lama? To answer this question we need to understand the Tibetan Buddhist belief in tulkus.

Tibetan Buddhists believe that esteemed, Awakened lamas have the ability to come back into this life to help bring others to the Buddhist path. So, tulkus are what other Buddhists call bodhisattvas—they are living bodhisattvas. Some people believe that the Dalai Lama is the only one in the Tibetan tradition who is said to reincarnate in this way, but that is not correct—there are significant others.

Tenzin Gyatso is the fourteenth Dalai Lama, and he is believed to be the reincarnation of the previous Dalai Lamas. He is also regarded as the living representation of Avalokiteśvara, the bodhisattva of compassion.

Tibetan Buddhists believe that the current Dalai Lama will provide information as to where his (or her) next rebirth will occur. (Although there have only been male Dalai Lamas of Tibetan origin to date, there is nothing that would preclude the next Dalai Lama from being female and/or of a different nationality.) Lamas[98] may have prophetic dreams that provide additional instructions, and after the mourning period following the death of a Dalai Lama, the search begins for his new embodied form.

Using the clues they have received, the search party will eventually identify a child candidate who will be tested. The test might include asking the candidate to identify objects or persons from his previous life. Once identified, the new Dalai Lama has traditionally been installed in his new home, Potala Palace in Lhasa, the capital of Tibet, and his monastic education begins. When the Dalai Lama came of age, he also became the secular head of Tibet.

The current Dalai Lama, as you may know, does not live in his traditional home in Potala Palace. This is due to the 1959 Chinese occupation of Tibet, which forced the current Dalai Lama to flee into exile. The Chinese government claimed and continues to claim that they are the rightful owners of Tibet because, they say, it historically belonged to China. They further claimed that Tibet's theocratic (religiously ruled) government was oppressing its people and making them "backward"; hence, Tibet needed liberation.

Tibet received no substantial help from the world community because other nations were fearful of upsetting China. China took control of Tibet and moved many of its own citizens there, and there are now more ethnic Chinese living in Tibet than ethnic Tibetans. What was once the most overtly Buddhist country in the world became one where religious practice was curtailed, monks and nuns were defrocked, and temples were destroyed or abandoned. While the degree of religious oppression has been slightly reduced, the country of Tibet is but a shell of its former Buddhist self.

Fortunately, the Dalai Lama escaped into neighboring India, where Dharamsala serves as his residence and as a center for Tibetan Buddhism. The Dalai Lama and the other Tibetan exiles continue to hope that they will be able to return to Tibet someday. In the meantime, one cannot help but admire the way in which they have managed their exile. They have garnered political support for their cause, built Buddhist educational institutions, and taken a very proactive stance toward preserving Tibetan culture in exile.

While not condoning the Chinese aggression, it is safe to say that Tibetan Buddhism would not have the global presence it now enjoys had not the tradition been forced to adapt to this new situation. The personal popularity of the Dalai Lama has enhanced the status of Tibetan Buddhism in the West. Today, American and European bookstores carry best-selling books by the Dalai Lama and other Tibetan Buddhist teachers. In U.S. cities, one finds Tibetan religious centers that have made not only Tibetan Buddhism but also Tibetan Buddhist art, food, and culture accessible to a non-Tibetan audience. The Dalai Lama has won a Nobel Peace Prize; his public talks in cities like New York and Los Angeles sell out; in short, he has become a cult figure for many Westerners, both Buddhist and non-Buddhist, who appreciate the personal embodiment of his teachings on love and kindness.

Dipa Ma [99] (1911–1989)

Nani Bala Barua was born near Chittagong, in present-day Pakistan, in 1911. From early in her life, she was interested in Buddhist rituals:

Contrary to the custom of keeping small children away from monks, her parents allowed Nani to offer food, wash the monks' feet, and sit with them while they ate. Instead of pretend-cooking like most little girls her age, Nani seemed solely interested in creating miniature altars and offering flowers to the Buddha.[100]

At twelve, Nani was married. (Arranged marriages are customary in the Indian subcontinent; people may be officially married quite young, but they do not live together and begin raising a family until they are older.) Years after her marriage ceremony, she was sent to live with her husband in Rangoon, Myanmar. Rajani was a kindly and supportive man, and the couple fell deeply in love. Nani struggled with being unable to have children but her husband consoled her saying that she should instead treat every person she met as if he or she were her only child. She kept this advice close to her heart for the rest of her life.

When Nani's mother died suddenly, she and Rajani raised Nani's youngest brother, Bijoy, as their own child. At thirty-five, that is, at approximately the age at which the Buddha experienced Awakening, Nani did become pregnant, yet her infant daughter soon died. At thirty-nine, she again became pregnant. When the baby girl was born, Nani called her "Dipa," meaning "light." It was at this time that Nani came to be called "Dipa Ma," which means "the mother of Dipa."

Hypertension accompanied these births and Dipa Ma came close to death. She had to lie in bed for several years while her husband struggled to maintain his job as an engineer and care for both his wife and the baby alone. At the age of fifty-nine, he died of a heart attack. This desperate situation occasioned Dipa Ma's entry into a meditation center. She believed it was the only way to save her life. Encouraged by a dream in which she encountered the Buddha, she began her practice.

She then went through a phase of entering and leaving meditation centers, balancing her own practice with caring for her daughter. Her health improved and she had an Awakening experience that she came later to describe in this way: "My outlook has changed greatly. Before I was too attached to everything. I was possessive. I wanted things. But now it feels like I'm floating, detached; I am here, but I don't want things. I don't want to possess anything. *I'm living—that's all. That's enough.*" [101] She also became quite adept at supernormal powers (siddhis).

Over time, her fame in Myanmar spread. Even after she moved to Calcutta, India, she continued to attract students, particularly middle-aged women like herself. She believed that women practitioners actually had an advantage over men. She told her female students: "You can go more quickly and deeper in the practice than men because your minds are softer . . . Women's tendency to be more emotional is *not* a hindrance to practice." [102]

Her discipline was strict. She expected her followers to emulate her own lifestyle of little sleep, following the five precepts, and meditating several hours a day. They had to report their progress to her twice a week. [103] Despite this forcefulness in her practice and her expectations, her strength came from her loving-kindness (metta):

> She taught a *metta* (loving-kindness) meditation, emphasizing over and over again "the first thing is to love yourself." She advised, "You cannot progress by self-doubt and self-hatred, only by self-love. This is the fuel. Our mind is our friend. It is our own source of help. It is our refuge. Unless you have respect for yourself, you cannot proceed." [104]

Dipa Ma ultimately drew the attention of foreigners and was a strong influence on such well-known American practitioners as Joseph Goldstein, Sharon Salzberg, and Jack Kornfield. This connection resulted in a trip to the United States in 1980 where she helped lead a retreat. Dipa Ma continued teaching in her apartment in Calcutta until her death in September 1989.

Sheng-yen (1930–   ) [105]
Sheng-yen was born in Shanghai, China, the youngest of six children. At thirteen, he was able to enter a nearby temple

called Langshan. His recollection of this Ch'an temple was crisp and tart—he thought there really wasn't any genuine practice going on there. His mentor, Langhui, recommended that young Sheng-yen perform prostrations to Kuan-yin (bodhisattva of mercy) to help alleviate his karmic debt. He did so, and he reported that one morning while bowing he "was overcome . . . with a very refreshing and comfortable feeling. It seemed as if the whole world had changed. My mind became very clear and very bright." [106]

At sixteen, Sheng-yen was sent to a sub-temple in Shanghai. For the next two years, he performed Buddhist rituals for the dead; this work helped raise funds for the temple. Sheng-yen did not enjoy his assigned task, and he left this sub-temple and enrolled instead in the Jing-an Monastery in Shanghai where he could pursue more formal studies. At Jing-an he was exposed to Buddhist ideas of many different sects, which allowed him to continue his meditation practice. He did not receive any guidance on meditation, however, and he came to feel at a loss as to how to proceed.

In 1949, China came under the Communist rule of Mao Tse-tung (Mao Zedong). Sheng-yen joined the opposing forces, the Kuomintang,[107] and served with distinction for ten years. His time in the army did not dull his ardor for Buddhism, and he reported that he took time every day for meditation.

In 1958, Sheng-yen met two Ch'an masters, both of whom were to exert a tremendous influence on his life. Their names were Lingyuan (1902–1988) and Donghou (1907–1977). Ultimately, Sheng-yen received transmission from Lingyuan but it was through Donghou that he attained full monkhood. Under Donghou's gaze, Sheng-yen advanced spiritually but it was not easy—Donghou was a demanding teacher who worked constantly to keep Sheng-yen off balance:

> When I lived with him [Doughou] he forbade me to keep a
> blanket because monks were supposed to meditate at night.
> When tired, we could nap, but we were not to rely on the

comfort of a bed or blanket. All of these arbitrary things were his way of training me. Although it is hard to think of this treatment as compassionate, it really was. If I hadn't been trained with this kind of discipline, I would not have accomplished much. I also realized from him that learning the Buddha Dharma was a very rigorous activity and that one should be self-reliant in practice.[108]

In 1964, Sheng-yen entered a three-year, solitary retreat. He carried out two such retreats. In the second of these he began to write. After his six years of retreat, Donghou suggested that Sheng-yen pursue graduate studies in Buddhism in Japan, and in 1969 he did so. He acquired his master's and doctorate degrees while continuing his Buddhist practice in Japan. He expressed his indebtedness to Bantetsugyû Rôshi and the difficult practice he experienced at his temple in Tôhoku, which is in northern Honshû.

In 1976, Sheng-yen began teaching in the United States, where he still works to this day. He now divides his time between the United States and Taiwan, and in 1990 established the Dharma Drum Mountain center outside Taipei City in Taiwan, which serves as a graduate school, conference center, and a facility dedicated to Ch'an practice. He is the author of many books on Buddhism and tours the world providing dharma teachings.

Taitetsu Unno (1929–   )

In the early 1950s, Japan was still deeply entrenched in the trauma of World War II and the subsequent occupation by U.S. troops. Taitetsu Unno found himself studying at Tokyo University graduate school while waiting to matriculate into the Buddhist studies program.

Twenty-four years of age and a Japanese-American, Taitetsu was among those Americans who had been detained in detention camps in the United States during the war. In Japan, he felt like a "stranger in a strange land." He had befriended a philosophy student, though—a young man named Teruo. Together they had worked on figuring out the world in which they found themselves. Teruo suffered with frail health as the result of having had tuberculosis as a child. He struggled with pain and fatigue.

One night Teruo asked Taitetsu, "What is karma in Buddhism?" Taitetsu's response was abstract and academic rather than personal, and the topic quickly changed. The next day, Taitetsu learned that his friend has committed suicide. This plunged Taitetsu into a profound period of questioning:

> That evening, I stayed up all night going over the tragic happening again and again. Three questions loomed large in my mind. First, I wondered if Teruo was now happy—was he now at peace? I thought about this for a long time, but instead of an answer coming to me there was only silence. Secondly, I wondered what I would say to Teruo's mother. What is the one word of compassion that I could offer her for her painful loss? I wasn't looking for hackneyed phrases of condolence but truly uplifting words. But again, I didn't know—there was only a void. And thirdly, I kept thinking of Teruo's question to me—what is karma, really? As I thought deeply about it, I realized that such an objective question, having little to do with my own existence, would invite only empty, abstract answers, answers of the sort that I had given to Teruo the previous night. For a truly meaningful answer, the question of karma had to become more concrete: Who am I? What am I? Where did my life come from and where was it going? There was only a blank.[109]

Faced with these existential questions, Taitetsu turned to the writings of Albert Camus and Friedrich Nietzsche. He also explored the scriptures of the world's religions. He reported that "Some of this was useful on one level, but none cleared the confusion that prevailed."[110]

He turned at last to the tradition in which he had been raised, Shin Buddhism. The maternal and paternal side of his family had generated Shin Buddhist priests. His once solely academic interest in Buddhism now emerged as his personal interest:

MASTER YUNMEN

Master Yunmen (864–949) was an esteemed Ch'an Master. Urs App's book (*Master Yunmen*) includes his biography and a section describing his teachings. Here are some of Yunmen's words:

> *Every person originally has the radiant light—yet when it is looked at, it is not seen: dark and obscure. (Section 143)*

> *As long as the light has not yet broken through, there are two kinds of disease: 1. The first is seeing oneself facing objects and being left in the dark about everything. 2. The second consists in having been able to pierce through to the emptiness of all separate entities (dharmas)—yet there still is something that in a hidden way is like an object.*
> *[Views about] the body of the teaching also exhibit two kinds of disease: 1. Having been able to reach the body of the Buddhist teaching, one still has subjective views and is at the margin of that teaching because one has not gotten rid of one's attachments to it. 2. Even though one has managed to penetrate through to the body of the Buddhist teaching, one is still unable to let go of it.*
> *But, if one examines this [teaching] thoroughly, it's stone-dead. That's also a disease! (Section 193)*

> *Someone asked, "What is the fundamental teaching?"*
> *Master Yunmen said, "No question, no answer." (Section 30)*

> *Whether you are an innocent beginner or seasoned adept, you must show some spirit! Don't vainly memorize [other people's] sayings: a little bit of reality is better than a lot of illusions. [Otherwise,] you'll just go on deceiving yourself.*
> *What is the matter with you? Come forward [and tell me]! (Section 61)*

On May 10, 949, Master Yunmen died. In the seventeenth year after his death, a local magistrate had a dream that Yunmen's tomb (he was not cremated) was to be opened. This was done, and his body was found not to have deteriorated but rather, "the eyes were half open and glistened like pearls, the teeth sparkled like snow, and a mystical glow filled the whole room." (30) Subsequently, his mummified body was honored at the capital for a month and installed back in the Yunmen monastery only to disappear in the mid-1970s during the Cultural Revolution in China.

"All world religions grapple with these questions, but in my case, due to fortunate karmic circumstances, Shin Buddhism provides the answers that are illuminating, challenging, and constantly evolving."[111]

In the Epilogue of his book, *River of Fire, River of Water*, Taitetsu Unno provides the answers to his three questions:

> First, who am I? Whence do I come? Whither do I go? The answer is simple. I am a limited karmic being, full of ignorance and forever wandering, who has been endowed with a gift, the single thread of nembutsu . . . Second, what is the one true word of compassion? I realize now it's not so much the word but the source that is crucial. . . .
>
> From its [great compassion] depth, then, emerges the genuine word (*desana*) that uplifts all of life as is. It may appear as a single word, or an eloquent silence, or namu-amida-butsu itself. Finally, is my friend who took his own life happy now? Who is to say? As far as I am concerned, I have no choice but to entrust myself to the working of great compassion that vowed to work ceaselessly until all beings, even a single blade of grass, are liberated into the universe of boundless light.[112]

POSTSCRIPT

These glimpses are only a few of the many such accounts in print. More importantly, the stories of faith that are written in the hearts of Buddhist believers are as numerous as the stars themselves. Taitetsu Unno's story illustrates what Zen Buddhism teaches, namely, that one needs to write one's own story without a "dependence on words and letters."

10

Buddhism in the World Today

The past should not be followed after,
the future not desired.
What is past is done with
and the future not yet come.

—From Majjhima-Nikaya, iii 87.

Today Buddhism has a presence in every country in the world. The growth in interest and devotion, particularly on the part of young people, virtually ensures that it will continue to expand in number of adherents and influence. The two areas of the globe in which it is likely to continue to be most influential are Asia and the West. It should prove useful, then, to outline the current concerns of Buddhism in Asia and in the West. In a postscript, I will hazard some guesses on how Buddhism might evolve in the future.

BUDDHISM IN ASIA TODAY
India

Around the twelfth century, Buddhism declined dramatically in India. It has long been surmised that this decline was due to factors including a revitalized Hinduism and a perception that Buddhism emphasized monastic life at the expense of laypersons.

Buddhism persists in India, albeit not in the large numbers it historically counted. The name that is most closely associated with Buddhism in contemporary India is Bhimrao Ramji Ambedkar (1890–1956).

Ambedkar was born into the so-called "untouchable" caste (these people are now referred to as Dalits). With this birth, it is not surprising that he suffered much discrimination as a child. Despite this, he was able to go to college, and ultimately he was awarded doctoral degrees from Columbia University and the London School of Economics.

Despite these credentials and his professional position as a lawyer, Dr. Ambedkar still suffered discrimination and even physical violence against his person. He concluded that the Hindu caste system was the source of the problem. Consequently, he abandoned Hinduism and, after considering his options, chose to convert to Buddhism. He publicly embraced Buddhism at a large public function on October 14, 1956. He died in December of that same year. However, his conversion and his writings struck a chord with many other Dalits who also converted to Buddhism. What Ambedkar saw in Buddhism was a worldview very similar to that of Hinduism but without a caste system.

Trailokya Bauddha Mahasangha (TBM) is said to be an outgrowth of Ambedkar's work. It is closely associated with the Friends of the Western Buddhist Order, a global Buddhist organization. Besides working assiduously to convert people to Buddhism, this organization also works to bring assistance to disadvantaged people through educational, health-care, and literacy efforts.

Thailand

Thailand is a stronghold of Theravâda Buddhism, and the home of two of the more prominent Theravâda voices of the twentieth century. One of these belonged to Buddhadâsa Bhikku (1906–1993). Buddhadâsa Bhikku was ordained a monk at twenty years of age. He studied in Bangkok, then established the Suan Mokkhabalarama (The Grove of the Power of Liberation) in an abandoned temple near his hometown of Purn Riang. His approach to Buddhism was that one couldn't divorce personal change from social change. The forces that impinge upon us and create dukkha are the same for both, and it is only through seeing the interdependence of all things through study and practice that each individual and his or her society will reach emancipation.

Sulak Sivaraksa (b. 1933) was a student of Buddhadâsa Bhikku. He is a Thai Buddhist who actively seeks to apply Buddhist ethics to the socio-economic challenges in his home country and around the world. He is the cofounder of the International Network of Engaged Buddhists. He has written numerous books in Thai and English, including *Seeds of Peace* and *A Buddhist Vision for Renewing Society*.

Vietnam

From Vietnam has come one of the most famous Buddhists of today, Thich Nhat Hanh. Hanh entered a Vietnamese Thien Buddhist temple at the age of seventeen. Through his traditional

Buddhist study and subsequent formal education in Vietnam and in the West, he came to see the need for a Buddhist response to the Vietnam War. He founded the "Order of Interbeing" in 1965. Due to his determination to speak out against both sides of the Vietnam conflict, he has remained an exile from his homeland to this day.

Hanh lives in a monastic community in southwestern France where he writes, teaches, gardens, and works to help refugees around the world.[113] Thay ("teacher"), as Hanh is known to his students, was nominated for the Nobel Peace Prize in 1967 by a former recipient of the same prize, Martin Luther King, Jr.

Hanh's thought, as traced through his many books, speaking engagements, and workshops, has focused on central Buddhist notions such as the nonduality of all aspects of reality, compassion for all sentient beings, and so forth, but perhaps he is best known for his emphasis on cultivating mindfulness. Ultimately, mindfulness will lead to Awakening, but even long prior to that momentous event, he believes, all persons can benefit from practicing mindfulness in everyday life. Hanh is an important source of inspiration for today's engaged Buddhist movement.

Tibetan Buddhism

We have already spoken about the towering figure of the Dalai Lama, whose spiritual message and influence rise above the world's troubles like the Himalaya Mountains themselves. It is ironic that the tragic fate of Tibet at the hand of the People's Republic of China was the operative factor in bringing the Dalai Lama and his message to the world. Ironic and tragic, yet strangely beautiful, the crushing blow that sought to destroy this ancient tradition actually accomplished nothing more than to break open its parochial shell and release the life within to go forth into the world. It unleashed not only the voice of this one "simple monk" (as the Dalai Lama refers to himself) but the voices of many other Tibetan Buddhist writers, musicians, and artists. It also unleashed a powerful and still-expanding application of Buddhist teaching to global politics and global economics.

BUDDHISM BEYOND ASIA AND THE WEST

We began this chapter by stating that Buddhism has a presence in every country in the world today. There is Buddhism in Africa, South America, and other locations that we may not think of as Buddhist. Many of these Buddhist outposts are the result of the efforts of worldwide proselytizing movements, such as Sôka Gakkai, which have sought to spread the dharma to the seven continents. The extensive publications of Buddhist authors and translations of Buddhist works have also contributed to the dissemination of Buddhism. Finally, the Internet, which can be found in the farthest reaches of the world, and which has thousands of Buddhist-related Web sites, has generated a "virtual sangha" with incalculable numbers of members. Even many who don't see themselves as Buddhists are sympathetic to its message.

WESTERN BUDDHISM

In the West, as well, the Internet has superseded cassette tapes and pamphlets as a conveyor of the Buddhist message. The rapid expansion of publishers of books on Buddhism has placed books by the Dalai Lama, Sylvia Boorstein, Jack Kornfield, and Thich Nhat Hanh, to name only a very few, on numerous American bookshelves. Although self-identified Buddhists still constitute only a small percentage of the American public, this has all happened remarkably fast when we consider how Buddhism arrived in the West.

History of Buddhist-Western Contacts

Some people think that Buddhism came to the West in the middle of the twentieth century with the emergence of interest in Zen Buddhism, but that is only the most recent in a series of contacts between Buddhism and the West. It is possible that the Western religions and Buddhism met just prior to or at the beginning of the Common Era. Some have argued that there is evidence of contact with Buddhism in the Bible itself. Perhaps the most substantial of these arguments concerns the story of

Jesus walking on the water. While there are many stories of Buddhist adepts performing this feat, there is no similar story in the Hebrew Bible. It is certainly possible that contact between the Western religions and Buddhism occurred that long ago, because both traditions would have traveled on the same trade routes in Central Asia, at least by the time of Alexander the Great. But whether or not contact had occurred by the beginning of the Common Era, it almost certainly happened when Christian missionaries reached China in the seventh century. These early Christian missions in China died out, however, and Christianity would not return to this part of the world until the long Christian expansion that began with the Roman Catholics in the sixteenth century and is still continuing today with most current Christian missionaries being American Pentecostals or Evangelicals. Wherever Christians traveled in Asia, they were likely to meet Buddhists.

Western contact with Buddhism probably also occurred during the thirteenth century as a result of European travel to Asia initiated by the Crusades. Whatever exchanges there were probably involved European and Asian traders. Exchange of goods was often accompanied by an exchange of ideas; indeed, that is how most religious and philosophical ideas spread prior to the modern period.

During the Christian expansion that began in the sixteenth century, missionaries often traveled with commercial fleets. Through the tales of these early travelers, both sacred and secular, the intellectuals of Europe became interested in Asia and its religions, including Buddhism. We know that such notable European thinkers as Arthur Schopenhauer and Friedrich Nietzsche found Buddhist philosophies fascinating even though their understanding of Buddhism was limited. This continued fascination gave rise to groups of people who were interested in leaning more about Buddhism and soon study societies were formed, such as the Pali Text Society in 1881 and the Buddhist Society in 1907. Very soon, translations of Buddhist sutras began to be published in English.

Buddhism in Nineteenth-Century America

The American encounter with Buddhism was based on the European experience. With Buddhist texts now available in European languages, nineteenth-century American intellectuals like Ralph Waldo Emerson, Henry David Thoreau, and Walt Whitman used Buddhist ideas in their writing. As was the case among European intellectuals, their grasp of Buddhism was not completely sound.

In the middle part of the nineteenth century, an interesting movement was born that encouraged interreligious dialogue and study. It was called *Theosophy*, meaning "knowledge of God" or "divine knowledge." The founders of this movement were Helena P. Blavatsky (1831–1891) and Colonel H.S. Olcott (1832–1907). The Theosophical Society was founded in New York in the 1870s. It sponsored publications, trips, and the establishment of centers in Asia, thereby contributing much to the growth of Buddhism in the West.

Perhaps the most often cited date for the introduction of Buddhism in the United States is 1893. In that year, the World Parliament of Religions was held in Chicago. Three Buddhist nations were represented at the Parliament: Japan, Ceylon (Sri Lanka), and Thailand. As a result of this meeting, both Theravâda and Mahâyâna groups began sending missionaries to the United States. Perhaps the most influential of these was Shaku Sôen, a Zen Buddhist. Although influential in his own right, the "culmination" of Sôen's mission came with his students, most notably D.T. Suzuki.

Buddhism in the Twentieth Century

D.T. Suzuki provided the foundation for the emergence in the mid-twentieth century of such notable British authors as Alan Watts, Christmas Humphries, and Edward Conze. In the United States, Suzuki's work influenced a wide range of people, including scholars, psychologists, college students, and the educated public. At around the same time, the popular Beat movement and its vanguard writers and poets, including Jack

Kerouac, Gary Snyder, and Allen Ginsberg, brought their own interpretation of Zen Buddhist thought to many readers.

Zen was not the only form of Buddhism represented on college campuses in the 1950s and '60s. Theravâda, Nichiren, and even Tibetan Buddhism were present. This surge of interest in Buddhism was accompanied by the study of Buddhism as a world religion in many colleges and universities; an outpouring of texts, tapes, and public talks by and about Buddhists; and the establishment of Buddhist centers throughout the United States and Europe that fostered the emigration of Asian teachers to lead these centers. The Buddhist centers we see today are not these early centers but the next generation. The present teachers, many of whom were born in the United States or Europe, are designated dharma heirs of the first generation Asian teachers. (A dharma-heir is someone who receives the sanction to teach and lead from his or her own teacher.) These present teachers are, therefore, the second generation of Buddhist teachers in the West. We are also in the midst of a second generation of Buddhist scholarship. The first establishment of a formal graduate program in Buddhist Studies was at the University of Wisconsin in 1965. Now many of the major universities in the West, including Harvard, the University of Chicago, and Columbia offer such degrees, and the quality and quantity of Buddhist scholarship parallels the growth of popular treatments of Buddhism, some of which are best-sellers.

It is small wonder then that the number of people identifying themselves as Buddhists has increased in the West. However, Westerners accepted the legitimacy of the study of Buddhism before they accepted the legitimacy of practicing Buddhism. The exceptions to this general rule were the early pioneers and the young persons consigned to the "counter-culture" of the 1960s. The generation after this embraced the emerging authority of Buddhism; its foreignness had worn off a bit by then and it no longer seemed as odd or as uncomfortable for middle-class Americans and Europeans to consider Buddhism as a belief system. It began to move from being considered trendy or attractively exotic to being just another viable spiritual option. It is clear that it has not wholly arrived at this juncture yet, but in the last twenty years it has made dramatic progress toward just such a status.

The growth of Buddhism in the West has not been without challenges and controversy. In the next section, we will assess some of Buddhism's current challenges as a prelude to our consideration of its future.

BUDDHISM IN THE FUTURE

Buddhism in Asia and in the United States stands at a pivotal point. We will begin with its position in the United States. The Buddhist mission here is facing several challenges. Donald Mitchell categorizes these challenges as "Ethnicity, Identity, and Practice" and "Authority and Gender" issues. He also notes and describes the promise of "Buddhist Ecumenism, Interfaith Dialogue, and Social Engagement."[114] Mitchell's categories can help us to begin to understand the dynamics of Buddhism in the Unites States today.

"Ethnicity, Identity, and Practice" Issues

There are two types of Buddhists in the United States. The ethnic Buddhists are those of Asian ethnic descent who have emigrated (or their parents emigrated) to the United States bringing their Buddhist beliefs with them. Buddhist converts are mainly Caucasian, upper-middle-class members of the so-called Baby Boomer generation. Which of these two represents "American Buddhism?"

The "conversion sangha" has developed highly progressive forms of Buddhism that are frequently divorced from the histories, families, and traditions that are at the center of the ethnic community. The ethnic Buddhist community is typically much more traditional. For example, in the Vietnamese Buddhist community the temple is the nexus for raising a family and the center of all social interactions.

Should American Buddhists do everything they can to keep their children in the Buddhist fold? "No!" say the baby

THE ART OF HAPPINESS

If you wish to gain a better understanding of how Buddhism is being taught in the modern world, you might try reading the best-seller *The Art of Happiness: A Handbook for Living*, coauthored by the Dalai Lama and Howard Cutler. The book shows how Buddhist teachings are being presented to contemporary Westerners, the vast majority of whom are not Buddhist.

The book sleeve claims that the book's contents are "based on 2,500 years of Buddhist meditations mixed with a healthy dose of common sense. *The Art of Happiness* is a book that crosses the boundaries of traditions to help readers with difficulties common to all human beings."

As the title indicates, this work purports to be "a handbook for living." Let's examine a section of the chapter entitled, "A New Model for Intimacy." In this chapter, Howard Cutler asks the Dalai Lama whether he ever gets lonely. The Dalai Lama, to Cutler's surprise, answers "No."

The Dalai Lama goes on to explain that he doesn't get lonely because he looks at all human beings in a positive way, at their positive aspects. In short, he regards all beings with compassion, which generates a connectedness between him and the other person. He states, "So, if you wish to overcome that feeling of isolation and loneliness, I think that your underlying attitude makes a tremendous difference. And approaching others with the thought of compassion in your mind is the best way to do this." (70)

Later in this same chapter, the Dalai Lama speaks about our interconnectedness. As an example, he invites us to consider the material objects we possess for the enjoyment of life; these are provided through the efforts of many people. For example, the book you are reading was made possible by the people who provided the paper, the ink, the publishing, the shipping, and, of course, the writing. He concludes, "So, despite the fact that the process of relating to others might involve hardships, quarrels, and cursing, we have to try to maintain an attitude of friendship and warmth in order to lead a way of life in which there is enough interaction with other people to enjoy a happy life." (74)

boomers who, as converts to Buddhism, obviously chose a different belief system than their parents. They will certainly teach their children about Buddhism, but they will likely expose them to other religions as well and allow them to make up their own minds as they come of age. At the same time, as Mitchell notes, the emigrant community is losing its sons and daughters to either the dominant Christian tradition or to no tradition at all. This situation does raise questions for both the unity and future of the collective sangha in the West.

"Authority and Gender" Issues

As you have no doubt noted, we have spoken almost exclusively of men in this book. Clearly, Buddhism has a long tradition of men being in positions of power. We saw that demonstrated in the status of nuns: the tradition considered them to be inferior to male monastics. This traditional gender structure was imported to the West, but it has come under criticism there by feminists. In addition, there were scandals in certain prominent Buddhist centers in the 1980s, and these shook the conversion sangha in particular. As a result, many prominent Buddhist centers have reexamined their leadership assumptions. They have made changes that, they believe, will allow all parishioners, male or female, straight or gay to experience the dharma equally. Male and female coleadership and rotating leadership are examples of such accommodations. This deviation from the traditional structure certainly seems supportable on the basis of Buddhist teachings, but the master-student relationship is to be built around the master's spiritual experience and not on his or her management skills or accord with diplomatic principles.

Buddhist Ecumenism

Part of the solution to these emergent challenges is the advent of Buddhist ecumenism. In Asia, where Buddhism was atomized into schools and countries, pan-Buddhist unifying efforts were rare. However, in the West, where many types of Buddhism are found together in a single country, there is an opportunity to think collectively and learn from one another. This might well hold the key to the concern about the split between the ethnic and converted Buddhist communities. There have been several significant meetings over the last ten years where participants worked toward reaching agreements on the common concerns of all Western Buddhists, and this bodes well for the future evolution of Buddhism.

Interreligious Dialogue

For more than forty years, Christians and Buddhists have formally come together to engage in spirited discussions about their respective beliefs and possible common ground. Through such interlocutors as Thomas Merton, D.T. Suzuki, Keiji Nishitani, John Cobb, and Masao Abe, this ongoing dialogue (which includes Jews and Muslims as well) provides a positive, new source for Buddhist globalization.

Socially Engaged Buddhism

One of the results of the encounter between Buddhism and the West has been a growing sense of social engagement on the part of Buddhism. Traditional Buddhist interests came closer to what we would call psychology than they did to what we would call social responsibility. Engagement with Christians, Jews, and the Western world in general has fostered a new sense of social engagement among Buddhists. This new direction has been inspired and informed by inter-religious dialogue.

There is, of course, a potential negative side to the Westernization of Buddhist countries. In a genuine dialogue, there needs to be a sense of equality and mutual respect. If one side assumes an air of cultural superiority, so that the other feels not invited but coerced to adopt certain ideas, then the basis of genuine dialogue has been lost and replaced by intellectual and cultural colonization.

While colonization is bad, the confrontation of ideas can be good. When confronted by the human rights values of the West, Asian countries have made changes. Sometimes, as in the case of the People's Republic of China, economic assistance has been directly tied to human rights expectations. With some success, Western countries have pushed the link between economic progress and achievements in human rights. Quite often, it has been the Buddhists within these countries who have risen to the social and economic challenges presented by the West.

The Buddhist Peace Fellowship, the work of the Greyston Mandala, and a vibrant hospice and prison ministry, are examples of how this new concern has born fruit among American Buddhists. Scholars like Christopher Queen, Kenneth Kraft, and David Chappell are documenting these efforts, as well as examining the kinds of doctrinal support that might be available for Buddhism to develop in this direction.

Buddhism in the Twenty-First Century
In the West

Buddhism is more than twenty-five hundred years old, but its influence in the West is relatively new. It does seem that Buddhism is here to stay, and it seems likely that it will continue to expand and prosper. Its challenges, though considerable, are not dissimilar to those it faced as it migrated from India across Southeast Asia. On this long-ago journey, Buddhism encountered new cultures with already established religious traditions. Its success on this journey demonstrates that Buddhism is a flexible tradition, and this bodes well for its success in the West. We may witness the development of new branches of Buddhism that cannot be categorized as either Theravâda or Mahâyâna in form. We will certainly see reinterpretations of the dharma as Buddhism settles into its new home, and these changes may well come with increasing velocity.

In Asia

Changes in the structure of Buddhism are occurring in Asia as well but at a slower pace. In the West, Buddhism is undergoing large-scale changes with very little traditional underpinning. In Asia, a thicket of traditional underpinning provides greater stability than Buddhism enjoys in the Western context, but it also puts the brakes on change. Perhaps this will allow Asian Buddhism to evolve less painfully and with fewer regrets. Certainly the large amount of Western experimentation provides Asians with a lot of raw data that they can use to formulate their own decisions about the future direction of Buddhism. It will be fascinating to watch what happens.

ca. **563** B.C.E. Birth of Gautama Buddha in Lumbinî (present-day Nepal).

531 Gautama Buddha renounces the householder life (The Great Renunciation).

524 Gautama Buddha gains Awakening at Gaya (Bodh Gaya); preaches the first discourse in Sarnath on the Four Noble Truths.

480 Gautama Buddha passes into *parinirvâṇâ* at Kusinara; the first council convenes at Rajagraha, India, and brings forth the *Tripitika*.

563 B.C.E.
Gautama Buddha is born in Lumbinî (present-day Nepal)

641
Songtsen Gampo introduces Buddhism to Tibet

480
Gautama Buddha passes into *parinirvâṇâ*; first Buddhist council convenes at Rajagraha, India

BCE (BC) CE (AD)

500　**500**　**1000**

C.E. 67
Buddhism introduced to China

552
Buddhism introduced to Japan

100
Theravâda Buddhism first appears in Burma (Myanmar) and Thailand

ca. 359
Buddhism introduced to Korea

380 Second Council convenes in Vesali over issues related to the practice as understood in the Vinaya Pitika.

271 King Aśoka's accession to the throne.

250 Third Council convened by King Aśoka at Pataliputra, India, with further dissension over doctrine.

ca. 247 Introduction of Buddhism to Ceylon (Sri Lanka), by son of King Aśoka, Mahinda, and King Tissa is converted; compilation of Buddhist scriptures by Aśoka.

1391
First Dalai Lama, Gendün Drubpa, born (title given posthumously)

1578
Institution of Dalai Lama formally established when Sönam Gyatso receives title from Mongol ruler Altan Khan

1300   1900   2000

1893
World Parliament of Religions meets in Chicago, Illinois

1966–1976
Cultural Revolution in China; temples, monasteries, and libraries destroyed in Tibet and China

1950
World Fellowship of Buddhists is founded in Colombo, Sri Lanka

1935
Fourteenth Dalai Lama, Tenzin Gyatso, born

240 The great monastery Mahavitara is established in Anuradhapura, Sri Lanka; Mahinda completes Tripikita commentaries in Sinhala language and *bhikkuni* order is established in Sri Lanka by Sanghamitta, King Aśoka's daughter.

C.E. 67 Buddhism introduced to China.

100 Theravâda Buddhism first appears in Burma (Myanmar) and Thailand.

200 Buddhist monastic university at Nalanda, India, flourishes.

ca. 359 Buddhism introduced to Korea.

552 Buddhism introduced to Japan.

607 Horyûji Temple built in Nara, Japan.

641 Songtsen Gampo introduces Buddhism to Tibet.

752 Vairocana Buddha statue of Todaiji Temple (Nara) completed.

779 Samye, first Buddhist monastic university (Tibet) is established.

805 Saicho (767–822) establishes Tendai sect in Japan.

806 Kukai (774–835) establishes Shingon sect in Japan.

1175 Honen (1133–1212) establishes Jodo sect in Japan.

1191 Eisai (1141–1215) establishes Rinzai Zen sect in Japan.

1224 Shinran (1173–1262) establishes Jodo-Shin sect in Japan.

1227 Dôgen (1200–1253) establishes Soto Zen sect in Japan.

1253 Nichiren (1222–1282) founds Nichiren sect in Japan.

1391 First Dalai Lama, Gendün Drubpa, born (title given posthumously).

1578 Sönam Gyatso receives title of Dalai Lama from Mongol ruler Altan Khan.

1591 Sen no Rikyu (b. 1520), founder of tea ceremony, dies.

1881 Pali Text Society is founded by T.W. Rhys Davids.

1891 Maha Bodhi Society founded in India by Anagarika Dharmapala.

1896 *Light of Asia*, published by Sir Edwin Arnold, generates interest in the United States and England in Buddhism.

1935 Fourteenth Dalai Lama, Tenzin Gyatso, born.

1959 Dalai Lama flees to India.

1966–1976 Cultural Revolution in China. During this period, temples, monasteries, and libraries destroyed in Tibet and China.

1970s One of the outcomes of the Vietnam War is an emigration of numerous Southeast Asians to the United States and Europe, which results in expanding the presence of Theravâda Buddhist centers in metropolitan areas; Insight Meditation Society founded.

1980–2004 The continued growth of Buddhist centers in the West; the expansion of the "cyber-sangha" with many Buddhist-related sites appearing on the Internet, including translations of sutras; the birth and growth of popular Buddhist periodicals (*Tricycle, Shambala Sun*) in the United States.

NOTES

CHAPTER 1: Introduction

1 *Theravâda* Buddhism is the more conservative form of Buddhism. It attempts to maintain the Buddha's teachings without historical change. *Mahâyâna* Buddhism, too, believes that it maintains the Buddha's teachings unchanged, but it claims that not all of the Buddha's teachings could be given to the world at once. What Theravâda considers "additions," Mahâyâna considers the "completion" of the Buddha's teachings, given when the world was ready to receive it.

2 Rebirth is sometimes called transmigration, or more popularly in the West, reincarnation.

3 Webster's New World College Dictionary, Fourth Edition, (USA: Macmillan), 976.

CHAPTER 2: Foundations

4 Richard Robinson, Willard Johnson, *The Buddhist Religion: A Historical Religion*, third edition, (Belmont, Calif.: Wadsworth, 1982), 7.

5 John Strong, *The Buddha: A Short Biography*, (Oxford: Oneworld Publication, 2001), 38.

6 Theodore de Bary (editor), *The Buddhist Tradition in India, China, and Japan*, (New York: Random House, 1972), 62.

7 Ibid.

8 Ibid., 63.

9 Ibid., 63–64.

10 Ibid., 65.

11 The deathless state, beyond the round of births and deaths, is called *moksha* by Hindus or *nirvana* by Buddhists.

12 Ascetics practice extreme forms of self-denial, including: sleep deprivation, taking only small amounts of food and water, denial of normal movement (sitting or standing in one position for a long time), refraining from talking, abstaining from sex, lack of material possessions, and homelessness.

13 Strong, *The Buddha: A Short Biography*, 70.

14 Ibid., cf. 74–75.

15 Ibid., 140.

16 One can distinguish between a human being and a human personal being. A human being may not develop into a human personal being. A human personal being is a human being who has consciousness of self (self-consciousness).

17 Masao Abe, *Zen and Western Thought*, (Honolulu: University of Hawaii Press, 1985), 6.

18 As quoted in Masao Abe's *Zen and Western Thought*, 4. Abe offers an excellent exposition of these lines in this book as well.

19 Ibid., 8.

20 Ibid., 9.

21 Ibid., 18.

22 Quoted in Thich Nhat Hanh, *The Heart of the Buddha's Teaching*, (New York: Broadway Books, 1998), 49.

23 Ibid., 50.

CHAPTER 3: Scriptures

24 The term *sutras* can be used in several different ways. The Buddhist scriptures are often referred to as sutras even though the Buddhist scriptures include much more material than what is contained in the *Sutra Pitaka*.

25 Donald Mitchell, *Buddhism: Introducing the Buddhist Experience*, (New York: Oxford University Press, 2002), 97.

26 Wisdom and compassion are the two primary Buddhist virtues. According to the Mahâyânists, the arhat demonstrates neither.

27 de Bary, *The Buddhist Tradition in India, China, and Japan*, 82.

28 See the discussion in Chapter Two on Right Livelihood, the sixth step of the Noble Eightfold Path.

29 de Bary, *The Buddhist Tradition in India, China, and Japan*, 155.

30 Quoted in Mitchell, *Buddhism: Introducing the Buddhist Experience*, 199.

31 de Bary, *The Buddhist Tradition in India, China, and Japan*, 198–199.

32 Jean Smith, editor, *Radiant Mind: Essential Buddhist Teachings and Texts*, (New York: Riverhead, 1999), 51–52.

33 Richard DeMartino, "On Zen Communication," Communication 8, no. 1 (1983), as quoted in Urs App, *Master Yunmen*, (New York: Kodansha, 1994), 53.

34 App, *Master Yunmen*, 54

35 Adapted from Mumonkan case 6.

36 The "Three Treasures" are the Buddha, the dharma (Buddhist teaching), and the sangha (Buddhist community).

37 Tantric Buddhism is based on esoteric texts called *tantras*. It makes use of diagrams called *mandalas* and magical formulas known as *mantras*. Whereas other forms of Buddhism view the passions as a hindrance to liberation, Tantric Buddhism attempts to harness and use the energy of the passions for the purpose of attaining nirvana.

38 de Bary, *The Buddhist Tradition in India, China, and Japan*, 331.

39 The shogun was technically the hereditary commander-in-chief of the Japanese army, but he actually functioned as the ruler of the nation.

40 As quoted in de Bary, *The Buddhist Tradition in India, China, and Japan*, 371.

41 John Powers, *Introduction to Tibetan Buddhism*, (Ithaca, N.Y.: Snow Lion, 1995), 219.

42 Ibid., 223.

43 Ibid., 233.

44 Ibid., 251.

45 Ibid., 452.

46 Louis Frédéric, *Buddhism (Flammarion Iconographic Guides)*, (Paris: Flammarion, 1995), 64.

CHAPTER 4: Worldview

47 Walpola Rahula, *What the Buddha Taught*, (New York: Grove, 1959), 20ff.

48 Ibid., 25–26.

49 Ibid., 26.

50 Keiji Nishitani, *Religion and Nothingness*, trans./intro. by Jan Van Bragt, (Berkeley, Calif.: University of California Press, 1982), 9.

51 Leslie Alldritt, "Masao Abe and Paul Tillich: A Dialogue Toward Love," in Donald Mitchell (ed.), *Masao Abe: A Zen Life of Dialogue*, (Boston: Tuttle, 1998), 238.

52 Sogyal Rinpoche is the author of a popular text on *The Tibetan Book of the Dead* called *The Tibetan Book of Living and Dying*.

53 Robert Thurman, translator, *The Tibetan Book of the Dead*, (New York: Bantam, 1994), 42.

54 Ibid., 45.

CHAPTER 5: Worship

55 http://www.cloudsinwater.org/home.htm.

56 http://www.cloudsinwater.org/meditation.htm.

57 Ibid.

CHAPTER 6:
Growing Up Buddhist

58 U Kin Maung, "A Buddhist Family in Burma," http://web.ukonline.co.uk/buddhism/kmaung.htm.

59 Ibid., 1.

60 Ibid., 2.

61 Louis Frédéric, *Buddhism Flammarion Iconographic Guides*, 186.

62 Ibid., 186–187.

63 Ibid., 188.

64 Cf. William LaFleur, *Liquid Life: Abortion and Buddhism in Japan*, (Princeton, N.J.: Princeton University Press, 1992).

65 Ian Reader, *Religion in Contemporary Japan*, (Honolulu: University of Hawaii Press, 1991), 89.

66 Ibid., 84. The Japanese employed earth burial prior to this time. Buddhism carried the practice of cremation of the dead from its Indian beginnings as it was and is an accepted practice of Hinduism.

67 Ibid., 84.

68 This account is largely taken from Billy Hammond, "Japanese Buddhist Funeral Customs," http://tanutech.com/japan/jfunerals.html, 1. This use of paper money seems an influence of Chinese spirituality where paper money (and other paper objects) are ritually burned to help those in the afterlife. The imagery of crossing a lake to enter hell obviously evokes the Greek myth where Charon ferries the dead across the river Styx that encircles Hades.

69 Ibid., 1.

CHAPTER 7:
Cultural Expressions

70 A.L. Sadler, *Cha-no-yu: The Japanese Tea Ceremony*, (Rutland, Vt.: Charles Tuttle, 1962), 1.

71 D.T. Suzuki, *Zen and Japanese Culture.* Princeton, N.J.: Princeton University Press, 1959), 273ff.

72 Ibid., 248.

73 Robert Fisher, *Buddhist Art and Architecture*, (London: Thames and Hudson, 1993), 98.

74 Vimalakirti is a lay Buddhist, a house-holder who demonstrates greater wisdom than Manjuśri. Manjuśri plays various roles in Buddhism, but here he serves as a symbol of Theravâda wisdom. The artists wish to convey the Mahâyâna belief that laypersons are as capable of attaining nirvana in this lifetime as monks.

75 Fisher, *Buddhist Art and Architecture*, 98.

76 Cf. www.uoregon.edu/~kohl/basho/life.html.

77 Ibid.

78 Shin'ichi Hisamatsu, *Zen and the Fine Arts*, trans. by Geshin Tokiwa, (New York: Kodansha, 1971).

79 Ibid., 31.

80 Ibid., 31.

81 Ibid., 34.

82 Ibid., 33–34.

83 As quoted in Masao Abe, *Zen and Western Thought*, 23–24.

84 Hisamatsu, 35.

CHAPTER 8: Holidays

85 Much of the material in this section is reprinted from "Japan's Obon Festival Reunites Families" (*The Brookings Register*, July 11, 2002, A7) by Ann Marie Bahr, with the author's and publisher's permission.

86 Pipob Udomittipong, "Thailand's Ecology Monks," in Stephanie Kaza, Kenneth Kraft (eds.), *Dharma Rain: Sources of Buddhist Environmentalism*, (Boston: Shambala, 2000), 193.

87 Susan Darlington, "Tree Ordination in Thailand," Ibid., 198–205.

88 This section is a slightly abridged version of "Chinese Ghost Festival Empties Underworld for a Month" by Ann Marie Bahr (*The Brookings Register*, August 7, 2003, A6). It is reprinted here with the permission of the author and publisher.

89 The information in this section is derived from "Tibetans Honor Fearless Female Bodhisattva" by Ann Marie Bahr (*The Brookings Register*, July 31, 2003), A6.

90 The information on Padmasambhava Day is derived from "Bhutan Honors the 'Second Buddha'" by Ann Marie Bahr (*The Brookings Register*, June 21, 2001, A7).

91 The following account of *Sennichi Kaihôgyô* is derived from the description of this ritual in *Religion in Contemporary Japan* by Ian Reader (Honolulu, Hawaii: University of Hawaii Press, 1991), 124ff.

CHAPTER 9: Memories

92 This section is indebted to Yûhô Yokoi's brief biography of Dôgen in his book, *Zen Master Dôgen*, (New York: Weatherhill, 1976).

93 Ibid., 27.

94 Ibid., 27.

95 The phrase "work out your own salvation" comes from Philippians 2:12 in the New Testament.

96 Ibid., 28.

97 Ibid., 32.

98 Lamas are high-ranking monks.

99 Interested readers may read more about Dipa Ma in Amy Schmidt's book, *Knee Deep in Grace: The Extraordinary Life and Teaching of Dipa Ma,* (Lake Junaluska, N.C.: Present Perfect Books, 2002).

100 Amy Schmidt, "Transformation of a Housewife: Dipa Ma and Her Teachings to Theravâda Women," in Ellison Banks Findly (ed.), *Women's Buddhism, Buddhism's Women: Tradition, Revision, Renewal,* (Boston: Wisdom, 2000), 201.

101 Ibid., 207.

102 Ibid., 210.

103 Ibid., 209.

104 Ibid., 212.

105 This section of the chapter is adapted from Dan Stevenson's biographical account of Sheng-yen's life in the book, *Hoofprint of the Ox,* (New York: Oxford, 2001) and Sheng-yen's short

autobiographical account found on the Dharma Drum Mountain Web site (www.chancenter.org).

106 Sheng-yen, *Hoofprint of the Ox,* 3.

107 The Kuomintang is the political party of the Republic of China, located on the island of Taiwan. It was formed by Sun Yat-sen, the father of the Republic of China, and led for many years by Chiang Kai-shek.

108 Ibid., 8.

109 Taitetsu Unno, *River of Fire, River of Water,* (New York: Doubleday, 1998), xxi, xxii.

110 Ibid., xxv.

111 Ibid., xxvii.

112 Ibid., 208–209.

CHAPTER 10:
Buddhism in the World Today

113 http://www.spiritwalk.org/thich-nhathanh.htm.

114 Mitchell, *Buddhism: Introducing the Buddhist Experience,* 338ff.

GLOSSARY

* Sanskrit (Skt.), Chinese (Ch.), Japanese (Jp.), Korean (K.),
  Pali (Indo-Aryan language used by Theravâda Buddhists)

âlaya-vijñâna (Skt.)—"Storehouse consciousness."

Amitâbha (Skt.) (Jp.: Amida)—Celestial Buddha of the Pure Land.

anitya (Skt.)—Impermanence, one of the Three Marks of Existence
along with anatman and dukkha.

arhat (Skt.)—"worthy one"; the one who has realized nirvana in the
Theravâda tradition.

Avalokiteśvara (Skt.) (Ch.: Kuan-yin; Jp.: Kannon)—Bodhisattva
of compassion.

avidya (Skt.)—Ignorance.

bhiksu (Skt.)—Buddhist monk.

bhiksunî (Skt.)—Buddhist nun.

bodhi (Skt.)—Awakening, nirvana.

bodhisattva (Skt.)—A Mahâyâna Buddhist term for the Awakened
person who foregoes final nirvana (parinirvânâ) and compassionately
helps unawakened persons to know the dharma.

Buddha (Skt.)—Awakened One.

Ch'an (Ch.) (Jp.: Zen) (K.: Son)—"Meditation"; School of Chinese
Buddhism that stresses meditation.

citta (Skt., Pali)—Mind.

Dalai Lama (Tibetan)—The head of the Geluk school of Tibetan
Buddhism; spiritual and secular leader of Tibetan people; current
Dalai Lama, Tenzin Gyatso.

dâna (Skt., Pali)—donations or giving to sangha (Buddhist community).

dharma (Skt.)—"Truth," teachings of Buddhism, law.

dhyâna (Skt.)—"Meditation."

dukkha (Skt.)—unsatisfactoriness, suffering; first of the Four Noble
Truths.

haiku (Jp.)—Type of Japanese poetry using set patterns of lines and syllables.

Hinayâna (Skt., Pali)—Lesser vehicle; a term that was used to denigrate and differentiate early non-Mahâyâna Buddhism from Mahâyâna.

Jâtaka (Skt., Pali)—the stories that recount the previous lives and activities of Gautama Buddha.

jiriki (Jp.)—"Self-power" (as opposed to "tariki"): the ability to realize Awakening through one's own effort.

Jôdo (Jp.)—"Pure Land"; the Pure Land School of Buddhism.

Jôdo Shinshu (Jp.)—the True School of Pure Land Buddhism.

karma (Skt.)—"Action"; the natural system of cause and effect that influences conditions of rebirth or Awakening.

karunâ (Skt., Pali)—Compassion.

kenshô (Jp.)—Glimpse or insight into Awakening.

kleśâ (Skt.)—defilements.

Mâdhyamika (Skt.)—Philosophical school of Mahâyâna Buddhism.

Mahâyâna (Skt.)—Major branch of Buddhism that stresses bodhisattva ideal, expanded canon, and enhanced inclusion of laity into sangha.

Maitrya (Skt.)—Bodhisattva of the future.

mandala (Skt.)—pictorial representation of the Buddhist cosmos used for meditational and ritual purposes.

Mañjuśri (Skt.)—Bodhisattva of Wisdom.

mantra (Skt.)—word or spoken formula used in Tibetan Buddhism for ritual or meditation purposes.

mappô (Jp.)—In Nichiren Buddhism, the idea of the last days for the dharma.

Mâra (Skt., Pali)—the tempter in the Awakening story of Gautama Buddha; symbolizes the challenges of the physical realm for all practitioners.

GLOSSARY

mâyâ (Skt., Pali)—Illusion.

mudra (Skt.)—"seal"; ritual hand movement or position.

nembutsu (Jp.)—Pure Land Buddhist term used for the phrase ("Namu Amida Butsu," Praise Amida Buddha) that believers recite (Ch. *nien-fo*).

Nichiren (Jp.)—Japanese school of Buddhism founded by Nichiren and based on his teachings and interpretation of the Lotus Sutra.

nirvana (Skt.)—to "extinguish"; Awakening, the Buddhist resolution to the problem of human personal existence, the Third Noble Truth of Buddhism.

parinirvâṇâ (Skt.)—the completion of nirvana at the point of physical death.

prajñâ (Skt.)—"wisdom"; the wisdom that comes with the Awakening (also *Mahâprajna* is used to distinguish from wisdom that is gained penultimately).

prâtimoksa (Skt.)—Buddhist monastic precepts.

pratîtya-samutpâda (Skt.)—system of codependent origination that explains the casual links between ignorance and rebirth.

Rinzai (Jp.); Lin-chi (Ch.)—Japanese Zen Buddhist school promoted by Eisai.

samsara (Skt.)—cycle of birth and death that perpetuates for all sentient beings until Awakened.

sangha (Skt.)—Buddhist community.

satori (Jp.)—Awakening.

Shingon (Jp.)—"True Word," Japanese esoteric Buddhist school founded by Kukai.

skandha (Skt.)—"aggregate"; the five constituent of the "self" (material form, sensation, perception, mental formation, and consciousness).

smṛti (Skt.)—mindfulness; part of the Eightfold Path.

Sôtô (Jp.)—school of Zen Buddhism championed by Dôgen.

Sthaviravâda (Skt.)—early school of Buddhism; foundation for development of Theravâda Buddhism.

stûpa (Skt.)—originally, reliquary or structure that contained sacred articles, bones attributed to Gautama Buddha; now extended for other Buddhist sacred articles.

sun (K.)—"meditation," Ch'an Buddhist school in Korea.

sutra (Skt.)—Buddhist sacred texts.

taṇhâ (Pali)—desire, craving of the ego; the Second Noble Truth of Buddhism.

tantra (Skt.)—esoteric tradition in Buddhism.

tariki (Jp.)—"other power," depending upon a separate power for Awakening (cf. *jiriki*).

tathâgata (Skt., Pali)—"Thus gone," term for an Awakened person used in Mahâyâna Buddhism.

Theravâdâ (Pali)—major branch of Buddhism that stresses the Tripitika, monasticism, and is the predominant form of Buddhism in Sri Lanka and Southeast Asia.

Trikâya (Skt.)—Three Bodies doctrine of Mahâyâna Buddhism.

Tripitika (Skt.)—"Three Baskets," the three parts of the Pali Canon (Vinaya, Sutra, and Abhidharma).

upâya (Skt.)—"Skillful means."

vinaya (Skt., Pali)—rules for the sangha; one of the three baskets of the Tripitika.

Yogâcâra (Skt.)—Mahâyâna school of Buddhist philosophy.

zazen (Jp.)—"seated meditation" in Zen Buddhism.

Zen (Jp.)—"meditation"; Japanese school of Buddhism that emphasizes meditation.

BIBLIOGRAPHY

Abe, Masao. *Zen and Western Thought.* Honolulu, Hawaii: University of Hawaii Press, 1985.

_____. *A Study of Dôgen.* Albany, N.Y.: SUNY Press, 1992.

About Buddhism
http://www.buddhism.about.com/cs/art/a./Art_Origins_p.htm.

App, Urs. *Master Yunmen.* New York: Kodansha International, 1994.

Armstrong, Karen. *Buddha.* New York: Viking Press, 2001.

Badiner, Allen Hunt (ed.). *Dharma Gaia: A Harvest of Essays in Buddhism and Ecology.* Berkeley, Calif.: Parallax Press, 1990.

Beck, Charlotte Joko. *Nothing Special: Living Zen.* San Francisco, Calif.: HarperCollins, 1993.

Buddhist Art and Architecture
http://www.buddhanet.net/gallery.htm.

Buddhist Festivals
http://www.echoedvoices.org/Apr2002/Buddhist_Festivals.html.

Buswell, Robert. *The Zen Monastic Experience: Buddhist Practice in Contemporary Korea.* Princeton, N.J.: Princeton University Press, 1992.

Carrithers, Michael. *The Buddha.* New York: Oxford University Press, 1983.

Carter, John Ross. Mahinda Palihawadana (trans.). *The Dhammapada.* New York: Oxford University Press, 1987.

Ch'en, Kenneth. *Buddhism in China.* Princeton, N.J.: Princeton University Press, 1972.

Chödrön, Pema. *When Things Fall Apart: Heart Advice for Difficult Times.* Boston, Mass.: Shambala, 1997.

Coleman, James William. *The New Buddhism: The Western Transformation of an Ancient Tradition.* New York: Oxford University Press, 2001.

Dalai Lama, and Howard Cutler. *The Art of Happiness.* New York: Riverhead Books, 1998.

de Bary, William Theodore (ed.). *The Buddhist Tradition in India, China, and Japan*. New York: Random House, 1972.

Dreyfus, Georges B.J. *The Sound of Two Hands Clapping: The Education of a Tibetan Buddhist Monk*. Berkeley: Calif.: University of California Press, 2003.

Findly, Ellison Banks. (ed.). *Women's Buddhism, Buddhism's Women*. Somerville, Mass.: Wisdom, 2000.

Fisher, Robert E. *Buddhist Art and Architecture*. London: Thames and Hudson, 1993.

Frédéric, Louis. *Buddhism* (Flammarion Iconographic Guides Series). Paris: Flammarion, 1995.

Fromm, Erich, D.T. Suzuki, and Richard DeMartino. *Zen Buddhism and Psycho-Analysis*. New York: Harper Colophon Books, 1970.

Gethin, Rupert. *The Foundations of Buddhism*. New York: Oxford University Press, 1998.

Gombrich, Robert. *Theravâda Buddhism: A Social History from Ancient Benares to Modern Columbo*. London: Routledge, 1988.

Govinda, Lama Anagarika. *Psycho-Cosmic Symbolism of the Buddhist Stupa*. Berkeley, Calif.: Dharma Publications, 1976.

Gross, Rita. *Buddhism after Patriarchy: A Feminist History, Analysis, and Reconstruction of Buddhism*. Albany, N.Y.: SUNY Press, 1993.

Hanh, Thich Nhat. *The Heart of the Buddha's Teachings*. New York: Broadway Books, 1998.

———. *Miracle of Mindfulness: A Manual in Meditation*. Boston: Beacon Press, 1987.

Harvey, Peter. *The Selfless Mind: Personality, Consciousness, and Nirvana in Early Buddhism*. Richmond, U.K.: Curzon Press, 1995.

Hesse, Hermann. *Siddhartha*. New York: New Directions, 1951.

Hisamatsu, Shin'ichi. *Zen and the Fine Arts*. New York: Kodansha International, 1971.

Jones, Ken. *The New Social Face of Buddhism: A Call to Action.* Boston, Mass.: Wisdom Press, 2003.

Kaza, Stephanie, and Kenneth Kraft (eds.). *Dharma Rain: Sources of Buddhist Environmentalism.* Boston, Mass.: Shambala, 2000.

Keown, Damien. *A Dictionary of Buddhism.* New York: Oxford University Press, 2003.

————. *Buddhism: A Very Short Introduction.* New York: Oxford University Press, 2000.

Klein, Anne. *Meeting the Great Bliss Queen: Buddhists, Feminists, and the Art of the Self.* Boston, Mass.: Beacon, 1995.

Kraft, Kenneth (ed.). *The Wheel of Engaged Buddhism: A New Way of the Path.* New York: Weatherhill, 1999.

LaFleur, William. *The Karma of Words: Buddhism and the Literary Arts in Medieval Japan.* Berkeley, Calif.: University of California Press, 1983.

Lopez, Donald (ed.). *Buddhism in Practice.* Princeton, N.J.: Princeton University Press, 1995.

————. *The Story of Buddhism: A Concise Guide to Its History and Teachings.* San Francisco, Calif.: Harper, 2002.

Loy, David. *The Great Awakening: A Buddhist Social Theory.* Boston, Mass.: Wisdom, 2003.

Mitchell, Donald. *Buddhism: Introducing the Buddhist Experience.* New York: Oxford University Press, 2002.

Nishitani, Keiji. *Religion and Nothingness.* Berkeley, Calif.: University of California Press, 1982.

Noss, David S. *A History of the World's Religions*, 11th ed. Upper Saddle River, N.J.: Prentice Hall, 2003.

"Parading the Tooth Relic: Kandy Esala" at http://www.pilotguides.com/destination_guide/asia/sri_lanka_and_ the_maldives/ kandy_esala_festival.php.

Paul, Diana. *Women in Buddhism: Images of the Feminine in the Mahâyâna Tradition*. Berkeley, Calif.: University of California Press, 1985.

Powers, John. *Introduction to Tibetan Buddhism*. Ithaca, N.Y.: Snow Lion, 1995.

Prebish, Charles, and Kenneth Tanaka (eds.). *The Faces of Buddhism in America*. Berkeley, Calif: University of California Press, 1998.

Prebish, Charles, and Steven Heine (eds.). *Buddhism in the Modern World: Adaptations of an Ancient Tradition*. New York: Oxford University Press, 2003.

Queen, Christopher, and Sallie King (eds.). *Engaged Buddhism: Buddhist Liberation Movements in Asia*. Albany, N.Y.: SUNY Press, 1996.

Queen, Christopher, Charles Prebish, and Damien Keown (eds.). *Action Dharma: New Studies in Engaged Buddhism*. London: Routledge, 2003.

Rahula, Walpola. *What the Buddha Taught*. New York: Grove Press, 1959.

Reader, Ian. *Religion in Contemporary Japan*. Honolulu, Hawaii: University of Hawaii Press, 1991.

Reynolds, Frank, Jason Carbine, Mark Jurgensmeyer, and Richard Carp (eds.). *The Life of Buddhism*. Berkeley, Calif.: University of California Press, 2000.

Rinpoche, Sogyal. *The Tibetan Book of Living and Dying*. San Francisco, Calif.: Harper, 1998.

Robinson, Richard, and Willard Johnson. *The Buddhist Religion: A Historical Introduction*, third edition. Belmont, Calif.: Wadsworth, 1982.

Sadler, A.L. *Cha-No-Yu: The Japanese Tea Ceremony*. Rutland, Vt.: Charles E. Tuttle Company, 1962.

BIBLIOGRAPHY

Sahn, Seung. *Dropping Ashes on the Buddha.* Compiled and edited by Stephen Mitchell. New York: Grove Press, 1976.

Santideva. *The Bodhicaryavatara,* trans. by Kate Crosby and Andrew Skilton. New York: Oxford University Press, 1998.

Master Sheng-yen. *Hoofprint of the Ox.* New York: Oxford University Press, 2001.

Smith, Huston. *Buddhism: A Concise Introduction.* San Francisco, Calif.: HarperCollins, 1993.

Smith, Jean (ed.). *Radiant Mind: Essential Buddhist Teachings and Texts.* New York: Riverhead Books, 1999.

Sogen, Omori. *An Introduction to Zen Training.* Boston, Mass.: Tuttle, 2001.

Strong, John. *The Experience of Buddhism: Sources and Interpretations.* Belmont, Calif.: Wadsworth, 1995.

———. *The Buddha: A Short Biography.* Oxford: OneWorld Publications, 2001.

Suzuki, D.T. *An Introduction to Zen Buddhism.* New York: Grove Press, 1964.

Suzuki, Shunryu. *Zen Mind, Beginner's Mind.* San Francisco, Calif.: Weatherhill, reissued 1997.

Tanahashi, Kazuaki. *Moon in a Dewdrop: Writings of Zen Master Dôgen.* San Francisco, Calif.: North Point Press, 1985.

Thurman, Robert. *Essential Tibetan Buddhism.* San Francisco, Calif.: Harper, 1996.

Tucker, Mary Evelyn, and Duncan Ryûkan Williams (eds.). *Buddhism and Ecology: The Interconnection of Dharma and Deeds.* Cambridge, Mass.: Harvard University Press, 1997.

Unno, Taitetsu. *River of Fire, River of Water.* New York: Image/Doubleday, 1998.

Wallace, B. Alan. *Tibetan Buddhism from the Ground Up: A Practical Approach for Modern Life.* Somerville, Mass.: Wisdom, 1993.

Wijayarnatna, Mohan. *Buddhist Monastic Life: According to the Texts of the Theravâda Tradition.* Cambridge, U.K.: Cambridge University Press, 1990.

Williams, Paul. *Mahâyâna Buddhism: The Doctrinal Foundations.* London: Routledge, 1989.

FURTHER READING

GENERAL INTRODUCTION TO BUDDHISM

Bercholz, Samuel, and Sherab Chödren Kohn (eds.). *Entering the Stream: An Introduction to The Buddha and His Teachings*. Boston, Mass.: Shambala, 1993.

de Bary, William Theodore, (ed.). *The Buddhist Tradition in India, China, and Japan*. New York: Random House, 1972.

Gethin, Rupert. *The Foundations of Buddhism*. New York: Oxford University Press, 1998.

Keown, Damien. *A Dictionary of Buddhism*. New York: Oxford University Press, 2003.

———. *Buddhism: A Very Short Introduction*. New York: Oxford University Press, 2000.

Lopez, Donald (ed.). *Buddhism in Practice*. Princeton, N.J.: Princeton University Press, 1995.

———. *The Story of Buddhism: A Concise Guide to Its History and Teachings*. San Francisco, Calif.: Harper, 2002.

Mitchell, Donald. *Buddhism: Introducing the Buddhist Experience*. New York: Oxford University Press, 2002.

Reynolds, Frank, and Jason Carebine (eds.). *The Life of Buddhism*. Berkeley, Calif.: University of California Press, 2000.

Robinson, Richard, and Willard Johnson. *The Buddhist Religion: A Historical Introduction*, third edition. Belmont, Calif.: Wadsworth, 1982.

Strong, John. *The Experience of Buddhism: Sources and Interpretations*. Belmont, Calif.: Wadsworth, 1995.

THE STORY OF GAUTAMA BUDDHA

Armstrong, Karen. *Buddha*. New York: Viking Press, 2001.

Carrithers, Michael. *The Buddha*. New York: Oxford University Press, 1983.

Strong, John. *The Buddha: A Short Biography*. New York: OneWorld Publications, 2001.

TEACHINGS OF GAUTAMA BUDDHA

Hanh, Thich Nhat. *The Heart of the Buddha's Teachings*. New York: Broadway Books, 1998.

Rahula, Walpola. *What the Buddha Taught*. New York: Grove Press, 1959.

Smith, Jean (ed.). *Radiant Mind: Essential Buddhist Teachings and Texts*. New York: Riverhead Books, 1999.

MAHÂYÂNA BUDDHISM

Ch'en, Kenneth. *Buddhism in China*. Princeton, N.J.: Princeton University Press, 1972.

Gómez, Luis O. (Intro. & Trans.). *The Land of Bliss: The Paradise of the Buddha of Measureless Light*. Honolulu, Hawaii: University of Hawaii Press, 1996.

Unno, Taitetsu. *River of Fire, River of Water*. New York: Doubleday, 1998.

Watson, Burton (trans.). *The Lotus Sutra*. New York: Columbia University Press, 1993.

Williams, Paul. *Mahâyâna Buddhism: The Doctrinal Foundations*. London: Routledge, 1989.

THERAVÂDA BUDDHISM

Gombrich, Robert. *Theravâda Buddhism: A Social History from Ancient Benares to Modern Columbo*. London: Routledge, 1988.

Harvey, Peter. *The Selfless Mind: Personality, Consciousness, and Nirvana in Early Buddhism*. Richmond, U.K.: Curzon Press, 1995.

Wijayarnatna, Mohan. *Buddhist Monastic Life: According to the Texts of the Theravâda Tradition*. Cambridge: Cambridge University Press, 1990.

FURTHER READING

BUDDHIST ART

Fisher, Robert E. *Buddhist Art and Architecture*. London: Thames and Hudson, 1993.

Frédéric, Louis. *Buddhism*. (Flammarion Iconographic Guides Series). Paris: Flammarion, 1995.

Govinda, Lama Anagarika. *Psycho-Cosmic Symbolism of the Buddhist Stupa*. Berkeley, Calif.: Dharma Publications, 1976.

Hisamatsu, Shin'ichi. *Zen and the Fine Arts*. New York: Kodansha International, 1971.

LaFleur, William. *The Karma of Words: Buddhism and the Literary Arts in Medieval Japan*. Berkeley, Calif.: University of California Press, 1983.

Sadler, A.L. *Cha-No-Yu: The Japanese Tea Ceremony*. Rutland, Vt.: Charles E. Tuttle Company, 1962.

WOMEN AND BUDDHISM

Findly, Ellison Banks (ed.). *Women's Buddhism, Buddhism's Women*. Somerville, Mass.: Wisdom, 2000.

Gross, Rita. *Buddhism after Patriarchy: A Feminist History, Analysis, and Reconstruction of Buddhism*. Albany, N.Y.: SUNY Press, 1993.

Klein, Anne. *Meeting the Great Bliss Queen: Buddhists, Feminists, and the Art of the Self*. Boston, Mass.: Beacon, 1995.

Paul, Diana. *Women in Buddhism: Images of the Feminine in the Mahâyâna Tradition*. Berkeley, Calif.: University of California Press, 1985.

BUDDHISM AND THE ENVIRONMENT

Badiner, Allen Hunt (ed.). *Dharma Gaia: A Harvest of Essays in Buddhism and Ecology*. Berkeley, Calif.: Parallax Press, 1990.

Kaza, Stephanie, and Kenneth Kraft (eds.). *Dharma Rain: Sources of Buddhist Environmentalism*. Boston, Mass.: Shambala, 2000.

Tucker, Mary Evelyn, and Duncan Ryûkan Williams (eds.), *Buddhism and Ecology: The Interconnection of Dharma and Deeds*. Cambridge, Mass.: Harvard University Press, 1997.

CH'AN, SON, ZEN BUDDHISM

Abe, Masao. *Zen and Western Thought*. Honolulu, Hawaii: University of Hawaii Press, 1985.

———. *A Study of Dôgen*. Albany, N.Y.: SUNY Press, 1992.

App, Urs. *Master Yunmen*. New York: Kodansha International, 1994.

Beck, Charlotte Joko. *Nothing Special: Living Zen*. San Francisco, Calif.: Harper, 1993.

Buswell, Robert. *The Zen Monastic Experience: Buddhist Practice in Contemporary Korea*. Princeton, N.J.: Princeton University Press, 1992.

Nishitani, Keiji. *Religion and Nothingness*. Berkeley, Calif.: University of California Press, 1982.

Sahn, Seung. *Dropping Ashes on the Buddha*, compiled and edited by Stephen Mitchell. New York: Grove, 1976.

Master Sheng-yen. *Hoofprint of the Ox*. New York: Oxford, 2001.

Sogen, Omori. *An Introduction to Zen Training*. Boston, Mass.: Tuttle, 2001.

Suzuki, Shunryu. *Zen Mind, Beginner's Mind*. San Francisco, Calif.: Weatherhill, reissued 1997.

Tanahashi, Kazuaki. *Moon in a Dewdrop: Writings of Zen Master Dôgen*. San Francisco, Calif.: North Point Press, 1985.

CONTEMPORARY BUDDHISM

Coleman, James William. *The New Buddhism: The Western Transformation of an Ancient Tradition*. New York: Oxford University Press, 2001.

Prebish, Charles, and Kenneth Tanaka (eds.). *The Faces of Buddhism in America*. Berkeley, Calif.: University of California Press, 1998.

————, and Steven Heine (eds.). *Buddhism in the Modern World: Adaptations of an Ancient Tradition*. New York: Oxford University Press, 2003.

Reader, Ian. *Religion in Contemporary Japan*. Honolulu, Hawaii: University of Hawaii Press, 1991.

TIBETAN BUDDHISM

Chödrön, Pema. *When Things Fall Apart: Heart Advice for Difficult Times*. Boston, Mass.: Shambala, 1997.

Dalai Lama, and Howard Cutler. *The Art of Happiness*. New York: Riverhead Books, 1998.

Powers, John. *Introduction to Tibetan Buddhism*. Ithaca, N.Y.: Snow Lion, 1995.

Rinpoche, Sogyal. *The Tibetan Book of Living and Dying*. San Francisco, Calif.: Harper, 1998.

Thurman, Robert. *Essential Tibetan Buddhism*. San Francisco, Calif.: Harper, 1996.

SOCIALLY ENGAGED BUDDHISM

Jones, Ken. *The New Social Face of Buddhism: A Call to Action*. Boston, Mass.: Wisdom Press, 2003.

Kraft, Kenneth (ed.). *The Wheel of Engaged Buddhism: A New Way of the Path*. New York: Weatherhill, 1999.

Loy, David. *The Great Awakening: A Buddhist Social Theory*. Boston, Mass.: Wisdom, 2003.

Queen, Christopher, and Sallie King (eds.). *Engaged Buddhism: Buddhist Liberation Movements in Asia*. Albany, N.Y.: SUNY Press, 1996.

————, Charles Prebish, Damien Keown (eds.). *Action Dharma: New Studies in Engaged Buddhism*. London: Routledge, 2003.

The Buddhist World

http://www.buddhanet.net/e-learning/buddhistworld

Buddhist Temples

http://www.japan-guide.com/e/e2058.html

Buddhist Corner

http://www.onmarkproductions.com/html/jizo1.shtml

Buddhist Texts

http://www.sacred-texts.com/bud/index.htm

Zen Buddhist Texts

http://www.sacred-texts.com/bud/zen/

Index of Buddhist Teachings

http://www.shingon.org/teachings/ShingonMikkyo

INDEX

Page:

6: Statistics adapted from www.adherents.com

B: © Leonard de Selva/CORBIS

C: © Gilles Mermet/Art Resource, NY

D: (top) © The Newark Museum/ Art Resource, NY

D: (bottom) © Réunion des Musées Nationaux/Art Resource, NY

E: © David Samuel Robbins/ CORBIS

F: (top) © Scala/Art Resource, NY

F: (bottom) © Brian A. Vikander/ CORBIS

G: © Brian A. Vikander/CORBIS

H: © Wolfgang Kaehler/CORBIS

Cover: © Kurt Stier/CORBIS
Frontis: Courtesy of the C.I.A.

LESLIE D. ALLDRITT is an Associate Professor of Religion and Philosophy at Northland College in Ashland, Wisconsin. He earned his Ph.D. in Religious Studies from Temple University in 1991 and was privileged to study with Dr. Richard DeMartino at Temple University. His current research interest is Japanese Buddhism and its relationship to the *burakumin*, a discriminated group in Japan. Born in Kansas, he currently resides in northern Wisconsin with his wife, Vicki, and son, Owen.

ANN MARIE B. BAHR is professor of religious studies at South Dakota State University. Her areas of teaching, research, and writing include World Religions, New Testament, Religion in American Culture, and the Middle East. Her articles have appeared in *Annual Editions: World Religions 03/04* (Guilford, Conn.: McGraw-Hill, 2003), *The Journal of Ecumenical Studies*, and *Covenant for a New Creation: Ethics, Religion and Public Policy* (Maryknoll, N.Y.: Orbis, 1991). Since 1999, she has authored a weekly newspaper column which analyzes the cultural significance of religious holidays. She has served as president of the Upper Midwest Region of the American Academy of Religion.

MARTIN E. MARTY, an ordained minister in the Evangelical Lutheran Church in America, is the Fairfax M. Cone Distinguished Service Professor Emeritus at the University of Chicago Divinity School, where he taught for thirty-five years. Marty has served as president of the American Academy of Religion, the American Society of Church History, and the American Catholic Historical Association, and was also a member of two U.S. presidential commissions. He is currently Senior Regent at St. Olaf College in Northfield, Minnesota. Marty has written more than fifty books, including the three-volume *Modern American Religion* (University of Chicago Press). His book *Righteous Empire* was a recipient of the National Book Award.